Building a *Life* Together—
You and Your Horse

Nurture a Relationship with Patience,
Trust, and Intuition

Magali Delgado & Frédéric Pignon

with Agnès Galletier

Translated by David Walser

TS
TRAFALGAR SQUARE
North Pomfret, Vermont

First published in the United States of America in 2014 by
Trafalgar Square Books
North Pomfret, Vermont 05053

Printed in China

Originally published in the German language as Die Kraft
der Verbindung by Wu Wei Verlag, 86938 Schondorf,
Germany, 2013

Trafalgar Square Books encourages the use of approved
riding helmets in all equestrian sports and activities.

Library of Congress Control Number: 2013956981

Photographs by Gabriele Boiselle
(www.editionboiselle.de)
Translation from French to German by Martina
Van Den Esch
Interior design by R2 (www.ravenstein2.de)
Cover design by RM Didier

10 9 8 7 6 5 4 3 2 1

Magali Delgado

Frédéric Pignon

CONTENTS

The Authors and Contributors viii

Acknowledgments xii

Gabriele Boiselle:
A Stroke of Fate xvi

Agnès Galletier:
Getting to Know
Another World xxiv

CHAPTER 1
The First Encounter 1

Why did you start playing with the foal
so soon?.. 3

Are there any guidelines for a first encounter
that will indicate progress toward a close
relationship? 3

What is actually going on at different levels
during an encounter between a person and
a horse? 4

So you believe that every horse needs to
be "started" again?......................... 9

What is your idea of a perfect environment
for getting to know a horse? 9

We talk of a horse "keeping his distance."
Can he give it up and open himself to a
human? 10

How can we ensure that the first meeting
with a horse goes well? 10

Keywords:
Intuition | Trust 14

Letter to *Fasto* 17

CHAPTER 2
Building a World
Together 21

Magali, whatever you do, you never seem to be
able to disturb Quelam. Is it the same with all
your horses?..................................... 23

How do you build that sort of trust with a
horse? Are there stages in the process? 23

And you, Frédéric, how do you approach a
new arrival you have never worked with?..... 23

How do you deal with a mature horse that
has only known other barns and riders? 26

At what moment do you feel you have achieved
the right basis for a good relationship?.......... 26

Besides mutual trust, what conditions are
needed in order to further the training? 29

Even so, you have deadlines to keep, in
the context of your shows. How do you
cope with these?............................... 29

How do you find the balance between asking
too much or too little of the horse? 29

In order to have a lasting relationship with
a horse, do you have to be on the lookout
all the time?....................................... 30

When do you feel completely at one with your
horse? What is the ideal relationship? 35

And so we must touch on the last phase of
a relationship, and finally on death................ 35

Keywords:
Patience |
Communication.................. 70

Letter to *Mandarin* ... 72

FOREWORD BY AGNÈS GALLETIER

CHAPTER 3

Growing Up Together 47

Magali, don't you find that Bandolero seems just like a member of your family walking along beside you like that?............................49

In fact is it the horses that have been your teachers?...49

Have the lessons you have learned affected your relationships with people? 49

Does a horse also change character as a result of human contact? 53

Have you ever been disappointed by a horse? 54

Keywords:
Openness | Rigor 56
Letter to *Dao* 59

CHAPTER 4

Losing and Finding Yourself Again 63

Are you still devastated when you see a photo of Templado? 67

Magali, tell me about Dao's death if you can 67

Are you not tempted occasionally to project a relationship, lost through death, onto a new horse?..68

Once you have established a good relationship, is it possible to lose it even though you are riding the horse every day?..68

How can one find a solution to avoiding boredom with daily routines? 75

What practical advice can you give to someone who feels the quality of a relationship diminishing? 76

When a horse is no longer being worked, how do you keep up the relationship? 77

Sometimes, it is us who cannot, either for professional or personal reasons, give the same amount of time to our horse. In this case, how do we avoid breaking off the relationship? 78

Keywords:
Risk Taking | Abandonment.....................82
Letter to *Templado* 85

CHAPTER 5

The Strength of Connection 89

Magali, how do you explain that your connection with the horses is so strong that you appear to be the focus of their lives and interests? 91

Frédéric, how do your relations with the horses affect you at the deepest level?..........91

What is it that attracts humans to horses? 92

What is the most important thing that horses have given you? 94

What are the reasons behind putting on your shows?..97

What do you consider is the message you are trying to get across to the audience? 98

Do you think that the horse has a meaningful role in our modern world?..........98

Keywords:
Sense | Talent 104
Letter to Our *Loved Ones* 109

Linda
Tellington-Jones 112

David Walser:
Afterword 120

THE AUTHORS & CONTRIBUTORS

MAGALI DELGADO

Born into a family devoted to riding and raising horses, Magali was already, at a very tender age, perched on the saddle in front of her mother as they took part in small horse shows. It was not long before she had her own horse and was giving displays to enchanted audiences. When she speaks, she often flicks back her fine auburn hair tied in a familiar ponytail, and her large, dark eyes radiate energy that comes across both to humans and to animals. She seems to be at one with her horses' feelings and thoughts and when she is competing, she is so concentrated on them that the outside world ceases to exist. Her father, Pierrot, recognized his daughter's talent at an early age and made sure she had the best education to develop it. Her success in numerous international competitions speaks for the wisdom of her approach to training, based as it is on understanding. Today, she takes her horses to major European horse shows like *Equitana* in Essen and *Salon du Cheval* in Paris. Sometimes she performs on her own and at others she combines with her husband Frédéric. It is always central to her performances that human and horse both enjoy whatever they do.

FRÉDÉRIC PIGNON

From his early childhood Frédéric was striving to understand the minds of horses and to build relationships based on respect in order to achieve his aims. He began his career by performing stunts but soon developed his unique ability to work with stallions in total freedom. He has become world renowned for his performances, which never fail to affect his audience and often leave them deeply moved. For five years he and Magali traveled the United States and European cities with the horse "spectacular" called *Cavalia*. In it they demonstrated what horses can do in a performance at liberty without any specific direction from a human.

At a young age, Frédéric and Magali discovered their affinity for each other, and the love that resulted was shared with their horses as much as between each other. This love and harmony now embraces their little son, Noah. They live together with their horses and animals in the South of France and are helped by Magali's parents who own and run a Lusitano stud that produces the majority of the horses they work with.

GABRIELE BOISELLE

She is a world-renowned photographer of horses, with whom she has been closely involved since her childhood. Her work has been published in numerous magazines and calendars and her love of horses comes across in a way that touches the viewer. She seems to get under the skin of her equine subjects and to see into their very souls. Her work is poetic, though at the same time powerful and dynamic.

She works in a building in Speyer am Rhein, Germany, that once housed her grandfather's working horses and she keeps horses that are the fourth generation bred by her "in the family."

AGNÈS GALLETIER

Agnès shares this love of horses and has done so since her childhood. Although she works as a journalist and has to cover every sort of subject matter, horses have remained her first and greatest love. The constant driving force of her books and articles over the years has been the desire to explore the relationship between human and horse and to bring the two closer in understanding and love.

Agnès lives and works in the south of France near Pau where she keeps her own horses, which include her 22-year-old Arabian Berber.

SUMMARY

When you read the biographies of the four participants in this book, it becomes clear that the common denominator of all four is the love of horses and a desire to make the language of horses understandable to the reader through pictures and words.

Agnès Galletier has managed to ask the right questions in order to draw out the instinctive wisdom, knowledge, and riches of these two extraordinary horsemen and to put it all into words.

Gabriele Boiselle has demonstrated by her intensely private pictures that images can describe emotion as well as any words, and they will leave you with a lasting impression. It has been a productive cooperation.

Thanks must also go to the German publisher, Isabella Sonntag, who has created the stage on which the play of words and pictures evolved.

Thank You

Gabriele Boiselle has been an honored guest in our house in Provence and at our shows for many a year. Since we first met she has built up a remarkable collection of photographs that capture something of our lives together and our relationships with the horses. She is an artist and we value her sensitivity and talent. Her pictures manage to express the individual character of a horse as well as his relationship with the person. For a long time we have dreamed of producing a book of pictures that would do justice to her talent and to what we feel we have achieved.

Who could we find to write the appropriate text to accompany these photographs? When we met Agnès Galletier over dinner at Magali's parents' house, we had no further doubts. She was the one. She entered the circle of our lives with great sensitivity. In simple and precise words we knew she could extract from our long talks the essence of our lives with one another and with our horses.

Thanks to Agnès' text and Gabriele's photographs, this book has taken shape. It gives a vivid picture of our stables that are the wellspring of our creative work and where the preparation for the shows takes place. The book also captures a little of the calm atmosphere of this oasis in which a friendly and trusting relationship is developed with each horse.

From this book you have in your hands, we hope you will derive insight into the way we live and our experiences. We hope you will derive pleasure and perhaps be inspired to explore a new and deeper relationship with your own horse and learn what this might bring to both your lives.

With love and appreciation,

Magali and Frédéric

Merged together—
Frédéric and Templado!
Frédéric buries his head in the
stallion's magnificent mane.
They both enjoy a moment of
complete togetherness.

Frédéric listens to Templado's
breathing, becomes aware of the
horse's heartbeat against his
own chest and the pulse through
his fingers, and breathes in his
odor. They become, as it were, a
single entity.

GABRIELE BOISELLE

M

My first meeting with Frédéric Pignon had no clear purpose but turned out to be a stroke of fate.

I was at the *Salon du Cheval* in Paris, hurrying for an appointment that had to do with my new Calendar Collection, when I rounded a corner and almost collided with a horse. There in front of me stood the snow-white stallion, Templado, with his extraordinary mane reaching almost to the floor. He had no halter—he was free. He stared at me surprised but not at all shocked. I stood rooted to the ground and gazed for a moment into his large, dark eyes. Any preconceptions I had were abruptly forgotten: His charisma and his aura flooded through me like electric current. It seems a bit dramatic but he appeared to me like a white angel that disturbed my soul and would not let me go. Then I noticed Frédéric Pignon at Templado's side; he was helping to carve their way through the crowd. There was such an obvious bond between man and animal that it was clear that no kind of rope or chain would serve any purpose.

Without a second thought I followed them; it turned out they were going to the same stand where I was to exhibit my calendar and where they had to be for the signing of a new book about Templado. Mesmerized, I watched these two souls who seemed to be communicating on a level of their own and enjoying the process. Templado placed his hoof that had been dipped in ink on the first page, and Frédéric signed with his name. The white stallion moved carefully between the table stacked with his book and the racks of other books and seemed to appreciate in a lordly way the astonished looks of the public. He clearly enjoyed his togetherness with Frédéric and the attention it attracted.

I could not get the memory of this first encounter with Templado out of my mind, but it looked as though it would be some time before I could get to know Frédéric and Magali. They were on the point of leaving with all their horses for the United States where they were preparing a horse spectacular. Furthermore, they were planning to get married in the last week before leaving—on horseback, of course! However, with their customary kindness they put aside some time for me to meet them with

their horses to take my first photographs. The weather was not favorable and I was still working with analog diafilm (transparencies) but I treasure those first efforts. Even though we had just met, they opened their hearts to me and I felt an immediate bond. The beauty of their love for the horses and for each other shone out of them and is written on my heart. I longed to capture this magic chemistry but before I was to meet Frédéric, Magali, Templado, Dao and all the other horses again, they would be seen by more than two million people in the USA and Europe.

Each time they entered the arena something special would take place. The audience could not fail to appreciate that here was a relationship between man and horse that had nothing to do with conventional training but one that was based on a confluence of hearts and minds, on understanding and love, on respect and humility. Here were two people not working with their horses but celebrating their day-to-day lives with them, and this embraced both performances under the arena spotlight and daily chores in the stable.

I could not help but be fearful that this exceptional quality would be damaged by exposure to show business over an extended period. Would they come through the experience without losing something of this clarity? They did so as I shall now relate.

Cavalia, the show that Frédéric and Magali dreamed up, was an unbelievable success in the United States and Templado became a superstar. Frédéric had first noticed this dominant little Lusitano foal in the Delgado Stud when he was still with his dam and realized that here was a rather special personality. When he matured, he became Frédéric's teacher and his soul mate. He was a gift from the gods and he shone on their lives like a bright star.

Then there were the other horses, all relatives of Templado. In the unusual breeding operation that Magali's parents had built up, the horses were treated with the same respect and love as humans, and this produced an atmosphere of trust and understanding among the horses for their owners. Later on when Frédéric and Templado played their "games" in front of huge audiences, grown men were seen to weep at the beauty and emotional quality of the performance.

There was a show number involving three stallions including Templado that stirred the soul of everyone who witnessed it. Likewise, there were Magali's incredible dressage numbers in which she performed all the most advanced movements, sometimes with nothing but a loose rope around Dao's neck—and no saddle and stirrups. I'm sure that everyone who owned a horse and saw these joyous performances longed to have that much of a close and equal relationship with their own horse. I say "equal" because Frédéric and Magali appear to be equal partners with their horses, not dominant humans imposing their will on a horse, however willing the animal.

While in America I saw their performances in Seattle, Boston, and Los Angeles and we often had long discussions. My early hunches were fully confirmed: there was nobody like them that I had ever seen—before or since. Of course, they were pursued by the rich and famous and often had to make difficult decisions about their future and what would be good for them and their horses. Finally, Cavalia came to Europe and I was present at their last performance in Lisbon. Their contract at an end, they returned home to Magali's parents and the Delgado Stud with gratitude and relief. The years in the States and touring Europe had been a rewarding experience, but wearing. For many reasons, they needed to get back: to breathe Provençal air, to wander among the stud's horses and foals in the fields, to watch the new arrivals—in short, to renew their soul.

Frédéric and Magali had started their lives together living in a hut, unheated in winter, next to their horses. Their love for each other and for their horses had seen them through difficult early days. Now they had resisted all sorts of glittering offers and returned to their modest house and their roots. When I first visited them back in their home, it seemed as if nothing had changed, but we all knew how much labor and love those intervening years had required. Also, there was the fact of Templado's death: When I presented Frédéric with a large photograph of himself and Templado, printed on canvas, he turned away to hide his tears. Even though Templado's bloodline lives on in his offspring, I think not a day passes without Frédéric talking to him.

In a very similar way Magali was affected by the life, and then the loss, of Dao, her exceptional Lusitano stallion with whom she had achieved so much, and won worldwide acclaim and many top dressage prizes. They too had a relationship that was so close that Dao would surely have gone through fire for her. Magali and Dao won first prize at *Equitana*, beating the top dressage riders in the world, and naturally performing with saddle, bridle, and top hat, as required of all competitors. Most horses and competitors were no doubt exhausted by the demands of this competition but not Dao: That very evening Magali was performing on Dao in another part of Essen at the Hot Top Show. There, she repeated all the dressage competition movements but without saddle, bridle, or top hat. Many of her competitors and the judges came to watch and were amazed, giving her a standing ovation. One judge advised her to take great care of such a valuable horse as Dao and make sure his legs were bandaged after each training session. Magali still laughs at the memory. "Do you know what I do when I get home with Dao?" she asked me. "I take down the ramp when I reach the stable and set him free. He gallops off across the fields with all their ditches and rabbit warrens. He leaps about and rears up with joy. If I didn't let him free to do what he wanted, he wouldn't perform for me the way he does in competition."

When Dao was old he shared the lives of Magali, Frédéric, and their son Noah until his last day. He walked along next to Magali with her pet crow on her shoulder, and by Noah's baby carriage, peering in every now and then. Dao appeared to be keeping an eye on them all. He was free without any halter as they wandered across the meadow. He was free until his last hour; then he was free to go.

*I*t has always been good for my soul to stay with Magali and Frédéric, to eat together, and to wander about in the stable among the horses. At the same time, I have got to know Magali's parents, Joelle and Jean-Pierrot (known as JP), and also Magali's sister, Estelle. When you meet these special people and their horses you soon appreciate that this family unit is an essential component of the magic they weave. The Delgados' daily life has always been a story of physical hard work. When you shake JP's hand you feel the marks and callouses left there by the countless times cleaning out stalls. Every day of their lives, they have spent hours in the saddle or on foot working with horses. The very way they move and hold themselves is different from other people and the horses feel this. For instance, when they walk among the herd to care for the foals, they are accepted as a member. They always have the time for a word or two with any horse that catches their eye. It's only in this way that the relationship between them has become so intense and fruitful.

There is simply no magic formula as one might expect with famous "horse whisperers." What always strikes me as being behind their success is that they are unsparing in their gift of time. In all my photographs, either on home ground or away during their shows, I ask myself if I am capturing the beauty of their relationship and the intensity of their feelings—not just their actions.

In the first book about Frédéric and Magali, *Gallop to Freedom*, they both tell their story and talk about their philosophy and experiences. I have always longed to help produce a book that concentrates more on the quality of their feelings and love for the horses, and vice versa. This is why we chose the question-and-answer format for this present book in which they can talk spontaneously and intuitively.

Because it is only possible to do this in one's mother tongue, I asked for the help of my friend, Agnès Galletier. It was clear from the first meeting between these three French people that chemistry was working. In no time at all, Agnès was accepted almost as an intimate friend. I could quietly lean back and watch with wonder at how quickly their friendship grew and how effectively they exchanged ideas.

I was hardly surprised because Agnès and I had cooperated on several projects. I valued her love and knowledge of horses as well as the vivacity and spirituality of her speech and writing. She was a television journalist, and for years had been the chief editor of *Cheval Magazin* in France. She was the right person for the job.

There is still someone I must mention because she is an important part of the story. This is Linda Tellington-Jones (see p. 112). With her unrivalled knowledge of horses she has been a great help; Frédéric is always acknowledging the value of her contribution. I myself have known Linda for years, traveled widely with her in countries like Syria and Jordan, and cooperated over her books. She has devoted her life to bringing out the best in animals and people and her TTouch Technique is a veritable gift from God.

For over 60 years, Linda has been going around the world to help people with their horses; on our journeys together, we would often find ourselves invited to dinner, after which we'd end up going out to the stables to sort out a problem horse. I knew I had to introduce Magali and Frédéric to Linda and they were all drawn to each other immediately like a magnet. I managed to arrange this just before they left for America and *Cavalia,* and since then they have been in constant contact with each other. The first time all four of us met together, the conversation stretched into the night and as dawn broke, where were we but in the stables. Frédéric once told me that every time they really needed Linda's help, wherever they were in the world, she simply materialized; this can only be explained by her ability to communicate on a different level.

Now you have learned something of the background of this book and why it has been given this shape. Before closing, I must first thank Frédéric and Magali who opened the door to their hearts and to their world. With patience and humor, they supported my ideas for the photographs and, whenever possible, used them. My thanks also go to Joelle and Jean-Pierrot who welcomed me into the family and gave me material and spiritual support. I also want to thank Agnès for the text and her determination to marry the text and the pictures in the best possible way. Finally, my thanks to Isabella Sonntag who patiently guided the making of the book over a period of three years.

We are all beholden to Frédéric and Magali for showing how profound the relationship between man and horse can be. They remind us that we are all connected with one another. They and their horses touch our souls at the deepest level and bring out the best in us.

Gabriele Boiselle

Magali and Frédéric relaxing in the meadow with a young mare from the herd in which, of course, they are accepted as members.

They feel part of the herd and move about and behave as if they are. The horses feel the same about them.

AGNÈS GALLETIER

G
Getting to know another world…

There are paintings you never forget because they reflect reality and touch your soul. One, burned into my memory, is of a tall, slim man with long hair standing next to a magnificent white stallion whose mane reaches down to the ground. In another unforgettable picture, a young dark-haired woman with a ponytail is riding a fiery Lusitano stallion with the lightness of a feather. Now I know that the two people belong to each other: they are Magali Delgado and Frédéric Pignon.

When I began my career in the horse world at the end of the 1990s I only knew their names from having heard about their show *Dancing Horses* in the Dominican Republic. In Europe, it was Frédéric's brother, Jean-Francois Pignon, whose excellent "freedom acts" with horses had captured the public's attention; people were mesmerized by his joyous and trusting relationship with his horses. From earliest youth, the two had

worked together acquiring and developing their skills.

Frédéric and Magali spent years in the States where they played a leading part in the hugely successful horse spectacular, *Cavalia*. When they brought the show to Europe the citizens of Stockholm, Berlin, Madrid, Lisbon, Brussels and other cities were equally beguiled. With its beautiful sets, live orchestra, and dramatic lighting the shows were more of a work of art. Achingly fine horses galloped about the stage in total freedom. Stunt riders, artists, and acrobats filled out the performances in a way that had not been seen previously. It was a new dimension for shows like this and everyone was moved by the atmosphere of love that existed between the people and the horses.

It was only years later that I had the pleasure of meeting and getting to know Frédéric and Magali. Our mutual friend Gabriele Boiselle asked me if I would be interested in supplying the text for a book based on photographs that she had taken of the two of them and their horses over many years. The photographs breathed affectionate admiration. Whether Magali and Frédéric were working with their horses or just at home, they radiated warmth and emotion. The book was to explore the relation-

ship, based on love, between man and horse, principally through the pictures.

As I made my way in early 2009 to Monteux in Provence, the home of the Delgado family stud, I had no idea what to expect. Little did I realize that I would find myself immersed in one of the most interesting conversations about horses that I'd ever had. I did not know at this point that behind the walls of this old, recently renovated farmhouse, a success story was unfolding that had nothing to do with fleeting fame. In this windy spot, rattled by the mistral winds, we sat on rickety chairs at a rustic table under an overhanging roof of traditional earthenware tiles. We were soon immersed in a conversation in which every word and gesture on the subject of horses was taken seriously.

After being welcomed by Magali's parents, Joelle and Jean-Pierrot Delgado, we met Magali's sister, Estelle, and were seated round the table to the sound of meat being grilled in the background, and enjoyed a typical Provençal dinner.

It was an easy matter to engage in conversation with Frédéric. Gabriele had already made the introductions and paved the way.

I was expecting to hear a history of Frédéric's experiences, his shows, trips, and projects but it wasn't like that; Frédéric embarked on the tale of his 10 extraordinary years with Templado and the terrible sense of loss at his death. He told me about their difficult early years followed by a time of joy and total trust in which intuitive communication engendered a feeling of the deepest love and affection. He touched on the feeling of desolation when Templado died and the emptiness it had left in his heart. He was frank and open with me, speaking about his convictions, his feelings and his doubts. At the same time, I sensed his shyness combined with a profound sensibility. Here was a story of a man, often beset with difficulties, whose fortune was shaped and guided by his horses. Every step he took was dictated by his determination to be honest, open, and loving with them, as he would with his family.

At our first meeting he drew out my own experiences in which my professional and private contact with horses had led me first to understand, then to write about, the role of horses in man's life. I told him I believed that horses could show man the way to lead a better life and to bring out his finer qualities.

I can hardly remember what we ate that evening because of the intensity of the conversation. I do remember that he began to develop and explain the feelings I had had for years about the relationship between man and horse. I knew that everything he said came from his heart and from his innermost feelings. At last I found myself in a place where I could speak openly about these thoughts that had been occupying my mind but which I always felt I had to be circumspect about sharing with others in order to avoid misunderstandings.

The next morning, after a night in one of the Delgado's guest rooms decorated with Frédéric's spirited drawings and paintings of horses, we met again in the stable block where Frédéric and Magali worked and lived with their horses. I had expected a stately Provençal building but found myself in a modest stable block built around a courtyard. Beyond was a sand-filled arena for training and in the open entrance area stood a table that was clearly the focal point of their life where they took their meals, talked and laughed and sometimes were joined by the horses.

Magali greeted me and invited me for a coffee. She led me into a small room that included an open-style kitchen, which was their home. There was no door or passageway that led to any other room. At that moment, Frédéric appeared and explained that they had converted four stalls into their living quarters: two for the kitchen/living room and two for the bathroom/bedroom. On the other side of the stable entrance that led to the central eating area were other boxes for the horses. Everything is centered round the horses and as we set out to meet them, we were greeted by an energetic neighing. All the stars of their shows were there: the stallions Fasto, Bandalero, Gracil, the copper-sheened Mandarin enjoying a good scratch from Magali, and the Friesian, Phoebus, kicking on his door to attract Frédéric's attention. Naturally, all the horses looked terrific with their glossy manes, well-developed muscles, powerful necks, and imposing figures but that was not what affected me most. It was the peace and harmony that shone like a sunbeam from the place. I had never encountered this before. The horses seemed positively thrilled the moment they caught sight of Frédéric or Magali. They peered repeatedly at visitors, tried to make contact, and often nudged them in a friendly way or touched an outstretched hand. It was a new day and they all seemed to be looking forward to spending it with their human friends.

It was clear at the most profound level that Frédéric and Magali are at home here. There is no frontier between man and animal, between work and private life, either by day or by night, in or outside the stable. Even when Magali is preparing a meal, she always has one ear ready to catch any noise that might denote trouble, and the same is true at night, when she is prepared to spring out of bed and go barefoot into the stable to check. "Living" for them means living with the horses—not to mention the dogs, the cats, and the crow that all seem to inhabit every niche of this Noah's Ark. An atmosphere of well-being hangs over this oasis. Each animal has his place, feels cared for and respected; this is what makes Frédéric and Magali so happy. In my experience, they are a rare couple, in that they live in such harmony between themselves, others, and the horses that surround them. Of course, they encounter problems and challenges like all of us; it all depends how they are dealt with.

For me it is no longer a surprise that Magali and Frédéric have impressed so many people. Those that step into their aura feel they have reached a bubbling spring. It is not only the horses that follow them with devotion and want to lay their heads on their shoulders. Their strength is the love that shines out of them and has a lasting, irresistible attraction, and it has nothing to do with fads or ephemeral success.

Agnès Galletier

Only when Frédéric is sure that the mother trusts him and is calmly grazing does he start to play with the foal.

The trust shown by the foal's dam rubs off on him and he becomes inquisitive and rolls excitedly about. Frédéric has to keep an eye out for the little flying hooves.

INSIGHTS
BY AGNÈS GALLETIER

Few people have the chance to know a horse they work with from the day of his birth. Frédéric and Magali draw their future four-legged workmates from the Delgado Stud so it was a privilege for me to accompany them one early morning to their favorite spot, the meadow where the foals were grazing. It was springtime and almost every day there was a new arrival to contribute to the family. This very morning another foal had been born and was standing with still unsteady legs next to his mother. Frédéric and Magali slipped between the mares, quickly adapting themselves to the rhythm of the herd so that they became a part of it. Whenever they came across a newborn, they took note of his level of curiosity and his behavior. They were particularly taken with a two-day-old foal that left his mother and courageously approached them in order to get a better look. Frédéric looked at him and then crouched down to make himself smaller. He invited him to play and, within moments, they were dancing as lightly as feathers blowing in the wind. It was great to see and Magali laughed happily as she no doubt took in a lot more about this foal than I did. At one point Frédéric was a bit too high-spirited and the little creature galloped back to his mother to nurse. It was obvious that for Frédéric it was love at first sight. The future will tell if anything comes of it.

The First Encounter

"The foal must give me
a signal that
that he is interested
in me."

Frédéric Pignon

Magali Delgado & Frédéric Pignon

Agnès: Why did you start playing with the foal so soon?

Frédéric: It struck me that his approach was a form of communication and I wanted to respond because he had aroused both Magali's and my interest. The purpose of this little game is to establish the degree of his interest in us and to learn something of his personality. We are always on the lookout for courageous and intelligent horses. This little foal, although a bit shy, captivated us both. This initial fleeting experience shared with him is perhaps the first step in a long journey together. The next encounter will tell us more.

Agnès: Are there any guidelines for a first encounter that will indicate progress toward a close relationship?

Magali: It is a matter of instinct. When I walk through the stable, I look from one horse to another without making any objective judgments about the character of each one. I have an idea of what I can achieve with each of them. I know their family tree and I have a fairly precise plan of what I hope to achieve.

The critical moment in a meeting is when a horse speaks to me in some way. It could be a look, the way he holds himself or invites my attention, and how he reacts as I approach him. Then perhaps a spark will jump across between us. There is a precise moment when a mixture of emotion and curiosity crosses the divide.

At the outset of any new relationship, there is the joy of getting to know someone and of doing things together. A horse develops his interest partly because he likes to play or just hang out with us. With very shy horses, a glance is enough to tell me what I

need to know: I get an idea of his nature and want to make contact even if it is not in the way I had originally planned. If there is a certain spark that tells me he wants to make contact then I know I have enough love and patience to create the right working relationship and achieve a good conclusion—even if it takes years. It is precisely this preparedness to devote hundreds of hours of work over many years that is important. If you have not felt this divine spark and do not believe strongly enough in the journey to devote all the time and love that is required then it will only be boring—both for you and for the horse—but, if you have felt the spark and have faith, then it is my conviction that the horse will always do his utmost to work with you and win your love.

In the event that you do not feel any goose bumps at the first encounter then I believe there is no chance of a good outcome. When I have found myself just assessing a horse's merits rationally, the relationship has always remained platonic. This is, of course, a perfectly reasonable basis for a good working relationship for some other people, but not for us. It would not be satisfactory either for us or for the horse. In order to be properly content, a horse must have a real attraction and be in the position to forge a firm bond. Without love at first sight, the equation is not complete and the best a horse can do is to be satisfactory, never brilliant.

Real talent is often not apparent at first, but if there has been this moment of magic connection, then unforeseen talent can emerge, not perhaps what we expected or even hoped for, but what is in that horse's nature. This is the contribution he will make to our lives and to our performances. The nature of this contribution emerges from the mutual attraction of man and horse and is often owed more to the horse than to the man.

Agnès: What is actually going on at different levels during an encounter between a man and a horse?

Frédéric: The first meeting with a horse is naturally of groundbreaking importance. It is perhaps dangerous to expand too much on the mystical aspect of it. My first meeting with a horse was imaginary and stemmed from my father's stories. He alone out of the twelve children in the family took care of the mare in the stable of the old farmhouse. From this contact grew a trusting relationship that he remembered forever, even in old age when he was far away from his childhood home. He was always full of praise and enthusiasm for the horses that had marked his childhood and he passed on this love and admiration to us, his children. In fact, horses had peopled our imagination long before we actually got to know any. At home, we thought of horses as embodying all that was beautiful, sensitive, and harmonious. I suppose that everyone, in a way, recognizes this symbolic contact with the horse: he embodies freedom and strength and seems to be symbiotic with nature. It marries our hidden animal strength with the ancient myths.

When I was eight years old, my father came home one day with a mare. Beside her I felt small; I was full of wonder but at the same time, I imagined myself to be a prehistoric hunter, clever and brave, who was going to establish a relationship with this animal and learn to master it. My brother and I watched every little movement of the brown mare, her efforts to approach us and, at the same time, we tried to approach her and to win her confidence so that after a time we were able to clamber onto her back. Once in the meadow that stood next to the house we began the process of taming her.

The two basic aspects of my getting to know a horse are the same for most riders: on the one hand, the little child meets this huge, motherly mass of flesh with a lovely warm hide, a pleasant smell, and rhythmic steps, on the other, he is the victim of this mad desire to tame and dominate the horse. In my opinion, this ambiguity contains the root of the problem. We are tiny compared to a horse and cannot achieve anything in an instant. In order to master the animal we have to learn to be modest and to rely on our instincts in order to succeed. Of course, the relationship will depend on what your aims are, whether, like Magali and

Frédéric gently strokes a mare.
Her foal watches attentively and
one can guess what is going on
in his mind when he sees this
strange relationship between
his mother and a two-legged
creature. He sees that his
mother is happy about it, that
she exhibits affection. The foal
moves closer in order to be part
of this happening.

He is conscious of the energy
radiating from Frédéric and
moves a little closer. Frédéric
finds himself smiling: This could
be the beginning of a new and
fruitful relationship.

8

myself, you want to build a close, trusting, and loving relationship or whether you want to train your horse for a sport. Whatever it is though, there must always be an element of intuitive as well as rational behavior.

Agnès: So you believe that every horse needs to be 'started' again?

Frédéric: Even when there are 30 horses in the stable and you have had as many years riding experience, you always have to be able to start again from scratch—even with a five- or ten-year-old horse that has already been worked. It is not a case of worming your way into the mind of a horse in order to develop his skills, it is a case of building a unique attachment—an attachment that belongs only to the two of you. In order to make a success of this you have to learn about each other, trust each other, believe in yourself and the horse (and vice versa) and thereby continually expand your ability to communicate. Without this, both you and the horse are stuck in your original state and there can be no magic spark.

Agnès: What is your idea of a perfect environment for getting to know a horse?

Magali: The very conditions we have at home! Thanks to my parents' breeding farm that is only a few kilometers from here we can get to know the foals as soon as they are born and we can visit them frequently. Out of the 15 or so born every year there is always one that catches our eye.

He is not always the most beautiful or the best built; he's the one that comes to us, the one that seems courageous or inquisitive. Of course, his beauty and gentleness, or the strength of his character can attract our attention. I remember, for instance, when Talento was only a few days old, he pricked himself on a thistle. He was absolutely furious and trampled the thistle into the ground. Meanwhile the herd was moving away so his mother called him but he paid no attention at all to her. He was all the more concentrated on destroying that infernal thistle. We were captivated and bet that his independent and combative character would suit our work. In the end, he

fulfilled our expectations and, today, this determined perfectionist puts every ounce of energy into the success of his performance.

When we get to know a foal from birth it allows us to build a special relationship with him from the start. Each foal has his own particular form of innocence and malleability. He is born with his own set of characteristics and this early relationship will help him come to terms with his nature. A horse that has begun life with bad experiences will not open himself to us so easily. He will keep his distance and we have to win his trust and prove worthy of his affection. Our little foals never go through that stage.

Frédéric: I always use the same approach with the foals in the stud as I do with dogs. I wait for them to seek me out. The foals that get close to my heart are the ones that come to me and show interest. It was what happened when I played with that little foal a moment ago. It is not necessarily anything to do with looks. It's the same when I'm buying a mature horse from another stable: he must first give me a sign. From the moment I see he is interested in me I believe he will find a place in our outfit, even though there may be a tricky start. Once we bought a one-eyed, rather delicate foal that had been called the "ugly duckling" at a well-known Lusitano stud where he was born. Without knowing why, we fell in love with him and today this horse is transformed and has a very special charisma. I do not know exactly why it is that one horse attracts and not another but I have always found that where there is love at first sight, the horse will find his place in our stable.

Agnès: *We talk of a horse "keeping his distance." Can he give it up and open himself to a human?*

Magali: Well, it has happened to me many times, but it has to start with the horse coming to me. He might display affection, invite a cuddle, or whinny when I pass his stall, anything that shows me I have been chosen as a partner. Then I can let myself be bewitched and look forward to an interesting and harmonious relationship. With an astonishing degree of intelli-

gence and subtlety, the horse indicates that he is about to carve out a space in our life and affection, and, in return, bring us joy. And it is all based on total trust that has nothing to do with daily treats or even daily handling; the trust comes more from the work we do together. I work step by step at each lesson, always taking into account his fitness and his mood so that the learning process becomes an easy matter for the horse. Pleasure in the work is my principal aim so I make sure to distance him from any source of ambiguity or conflict; I never forget the limitations imposed by his fitness or his character. There is never even a shadow of any "rigid" dressage training.

Once, for instance, we had a foal that was, at first, frightened to do any work when separated from his playmates. Instead of taking him away from the others in order for him to concentrate on me, which would certainly have made him panic, I worked with him next to the meadow where his friends were. Only when he had developed enough trust in me and learned to enjoy his work did I take him off to the arena. You always have to look for a

solution that suits the horse and not just use one that goes along with your principles or past habits.

When you are inflexible, the best horse in the world that was ready to work with you can suddenly refuse and become obstinate. A horse is full of good will; he wants to learn but it is up to you to find the way that suits him best. If you cannot find it the horse will begin to mistrust you and show anxiety. In the end, a trusting relationship is no longer on the cards.

Agnès: *How can we ensure that the first meeting with a horse goes well?*

Magali: First of all you need goodwill. For me, this means that the rider is ready to do anything for the horse. When you really believe this, that is, that you will have enough patience and love to lavish on him, this is the horse for you.

I might not have said this a few years ago were it not for an experience that taught me a lesson. We had a visit from a charming lady who was, how-

10

Keyword:
INTUITION

When it comes to horses, intuition is vitally important. Of all the people who come to us, there are only a few who know how to listen to their intuition. Women are, on the whole, better than we men; you have to be careful not to confuse intuition with impulsiveness. In order to build a sure and harmonious relationship with a horse, we encourage a rider to learn to trust their instinct. This is not easy for some people because intuition is a profound feeling that appears from nowhere but it suddenly seems to be absolutely clear and without compromise. When I have a problem, an answer arrives out of the blue and I know that it is the right one. We are all gifted with ways of receiving and understanding information as well as energy that we cannot really describe. Our subconscious takes in all this information and connects to a worldwide body of energy and knowledge. I think this is how intuition leads us into areas that remain closed to our consciousness.

When we are in the company of our horses we must always be prepared to listen to our intuition because our intellect and our human experience do not always supply the answers. Magali and I form our new horses more by intuitive decisions than by rational ones. It enables me to react on the instant to any situation without having to consider what to do. After a time it becomes automatic to relegate the intellect to second place, and this allows me to have lightning reactions and make instant decisions, even in life-threatening situations.

I'll give you an example: When Templado was near the end of his life, Magali and I both had the strongest feeling on the same evening that we should take him out of the clinic, against the advice of the veterinarians, and bring him home. As soon as he got into his stall he began to recover his energy and his love of life. I know we were right in what we did. Nevertheless I have to say that it is always a risky business following your intuition even though it is evident that you cannot rely just on experience and rational decisions. You may feel strongly, or be convinced about a course of action, but there is no guarantee. In our world full of rules and regulations, it can be an anxious business following your instincts until you have learned by experience to trust them.

Frédéric Pignon

Keyword:
TRUST

An encounter with a horse involves an act of trust on both sides. We hold out a hand and he, a nose, while each one looks at the other a little nervously. It takes time and several attempts to approach each other before trust and friendship can begin to form. When two meet, there are always two different personalities, two life experiences that are trying to find common ground. Care and trust must always be present when you enter this unknown territory.

However curious and interested the horse is, you have always to remember that he is a "prey" animal and, therefore, on his guard. When he is a stallion as well, the matter of hierarchy complicates things further. Trust is always central to a relationship but you must be aware that the horse is a living creature that can always have an unexpected reaction—even when you have known him and worked with him for years and can anticipate most of his reactions.

Even in the closest friendships you never know the other party totally, so there can always be surprises. With horses, I would even suggest that you seek out new adventures and experiences, for example, go on a long ride together on an unfamiliar trail, take part in a show, and meet strange horses in order to narrow the area that might bring surprises. One day you could both be old friends together and (almost) trust each other blindfolded!

Frédéric Pignon

15

Letter to *Fasto*

It was you who came to me. Even at our first encounter when you were a little foal, you looked me straight in the eye as if to say, "You interest me. Who are you? Can we do something together?" At the time we were busy preparing our show in the Caribbean and Florida so I could not really devote much time to you. However, each time we came back home on a visit, I would stand in the midst of the herd and you would approach me and hold my gaze. You were very determined and I said to Magali, "This foal intrigues me. He has an incredible aura about him and he is waiting for me."

We were away for many months on the other side of the world but when we returned I decided to make a study about the behavior of foals when playing with each other. I wanted to understand how the games began and how they came to a stop so I could use this knowledge when I played games with them. This is when I got to know you. I had already seen that whenever the foals began to play you were the leader, so I reckoned you were the one to help me in this project. I saw that you were the one the others followed. You ran in front of them bucking and behaving as if you wanted to engage in a fight. This display seemed designed to get them to follow you. Then you played with them just as in the wild but at a certain moment you decided the game was over. You stood quite still then began to graze. No one was allowed to disturb you. It had been your decision and you knew exactly how to enforce it. Everyone respected you and obeyed. This was the very example I needed for my work. You entered our lives and our troop of horses without a moment's doubt on our part.

Since you were Templado's brother there were no doubts about your charisma. From the start I had the feeling that I understood you at the deepest level. In all our games with the horses, you were the only one who took over from me as the dominant force. Just as when you were a foal, you did whatever you wanted and it was always carried out in your way and at your speed.

Though I was the trainer you turned me into a spectator of your excesses. For instance, in the middle of a performance you might suddenly decide to gallop to the other end of the arena throwing your spotless white mane about, have a good roll in the darkest sand—to the delight of the spectators—then come back to me and lean your head on my shoulder as if to say sorry for stepping out of line again. When I tried teaching you the Spanish Step it was hopeless but when you made up your mind to learn a movement like the impressive cabrade, you were the star. You taught me to make you happy so that your charisma could come into its own.

In this way you showed me what the essence of a good performance is, especially with horses, and you are the only horse that has, as it were, stage-managed our relationship. I've learned many things from you and now that you are retired here at home, I hope you feel you made the right choice and that, 15 years ago, when you fixed me with your gaze, it was worth waiting for me.

Frédéric

17

INSIGHTS
BY AGNÈS GALLETIER

It was a privilege for me to be able to immerse myself in Frédéric and Magali's world for a few days. I was completely free to watch them as they went about their daily tasks. I was trying to understand how this extraordinary relationship between human and horse translated into successful performances.

There was nothing spectacular about their daily routine, nor was there any magic ingredient. What I became aware of was a deep understanding between them, in which all of them listened and understood each other. The trust that this engendered seemed, as a result, to be quite normal. It could be that these two people behaved toward their horses as normally people do to each other in a family setting—or possibly better: a tender kiss for this one, a loving "Good morning" for another, attention to a little wound on a third. They knew the particular needs of each horse and the horses showed not the slightest tension. They greeted Magali and Frédéric with evident joy and each one received the special

acknowledgment he was expecting. What I witnessed made me speechless and filled me with joy. I had never seen anything like it in the horse world before.

On another morning, I sat by the side of the ring watching Frédéric at work with the Friesians, Phebus and Paulus. At the same time, I was keeping an eye on Magali who was mucking out Quelam's box. She was chattering away to the horse and interpreting the horse's thoughts in the most amusing way. Her talk was seeded with mimicry and laughter, and before she set off with the wheelbarrow full of manure, she gave the horse a good stroke and shared a thought with him.

Nothing seemed to disturb the calm: neither Magali's pet crow sitting on her shoulder, shrieking and flapping its wings, nor the cat wandering between the horse's legs, not even the pitchfork when it fell noisily to the ground. All was calm and radiating trust.

20

"I immerse myself in every
new enterprise like an explorer
in an undiscovered country.
I treat each new situation
without prejudice or preconception."

Frédéric Pignon

Agnès: *Magali, whatever you do, you never seem to be able to disturb Quelam. Is it the same with all your horses?*

Magali: No! When I'm mucking out, it's only with my old mate Quelam that I can have the crow flapping about and cat wandering in and out. I wouldn't risk that with a horse that had just joined our farm. Even the most experienced professionals need years to build that sort of confidence. It requires a lot of patience.

The relationship with a horse is not a straight road; there can always be the unexpected. You can take nothing for granted.

Agnès: *How do you build that sort of trust with a horse? Are there stages in the process?*

Magali: Yes! There are definitely stages even when you know all the peculiarities of a horse and know his rhythm. In the first stage you experience the horse's growing confidence. Then comes the effort to implement the resolutions you made, and the ideas you had when you first saw the horse. After the initial euphoria the reality becomes apparent: things don't turn out exactly as you first thought they would, and when you are not careful, you slip back into your old ways of thinking. It's the same between two people. After the first excitement of making a new acquaintance, you begin to learn about the other person then learn to live with what you know and to work out your way of communication.

When I start out with a young horse, I take time to study his character and learn about his fears. I also teach him what I expect from him and how we exist together in this place. I always go to pet new arrivals several times a day. I'll put on a halter, walk them around the stable; I show them the longeing ring, take them to visit the meadow, and also the place where we wash the horses in order to gauge their reaction. This lays the foundation for our work together and it is these little daily tasks that build trust. At the same time, I'm learning something about the horse's character so we are building our personal understanding of each other. After about a year of getting to know each other I'm careful not to vary my approach too much or introduce too many new elements. This is important because when we start working and the horse meets situations that unnerve him, he knows where he stands with me and also knows what my reaction will be in order to regulate his stress level.

Agnès: *And you, Frederic, how do you approach a new arrival you have never worked with?*

Frédéric: The thought of a new challenge always excites me. I try to imagine a blank sheet of paper or,

more appropriately, a canvas on which I'll begin a new picture. At this point, I am probably deluding myself because things rarely turn out the way I think they will. However, I am never nervous about it: I know that in my daily contact with this horse I'll discover faults that I had not noticed at first but also discover good qualities I had not expected. I enter into each relationship like an explorer in an unknown land, impatient to understand and make discoveries. If you begin the journey with fixed ideas about the character of a new horse, you might well miss his true and individual character. Worse still, you cannot then build a proper relationship and the horse remains miserably trapped in a dark cage, in which his talents lie undiscovered.

Magali and I had an experience that exemplifies this situation. We once found ourselves in Portugal with a group of people who spoke together in their own language and made not the slightest effort to communicate with us. After a few days—and fruitless attempts—we remained silent and hoped it would come to an end soon.

Guizo (left) and Phoebus (above).

It is the same with horses: If you do not attempt to understand their language and communicate with them, they simply dry up and often stand quite still or do only the minimum required. They are like an extinguished flame.

Agnès: *How do you deal with a mature horse that has only known other barns and riders?*

Frédéric: Contrary to what you might think, it is more difficult with an older horse because a foal has no preconceived ideas: he is curious, eager to learn, and you only have to control his stress when he makes each new discovery; not a difficult matter. Mature horses are already marked by their experiences—a past that we don't know about—both good or bad. Sometimes these horses are like an extinguished flame, as I already touched upon, or frightened. Some are so nervous that they will not enter their stall easily; they shy at the sight of a pitchfork or any normal day-to-day activities. In the worst cases, they are too traumatized to be able to analyze or

reflect on a situation; the mere sight of the trainer sends them into a spin. They are unable to respond to the simplest command and either take flight or, especially in the case of stallions, become aggressive. Hiding behind this aggression is simply a terrible state of stress when faced with a human. My solution is to return to base by immersing such a horse in the simplest daily activities. I feed him, stroke him, talk to him, brush him, walk with him on the longe line, watching all the time to see what sparks the loss of control. It is only through understanding the horse that I can begin to help him. Naturally, I draw on my experience and whatever facts I know about his history but I rely on my intuition to invent, with much improvisation, a new gamut of experiences that belong just to the two of us. This will be the foundation of our work together in the coming years.

Agnès: *At what moment do you feel you have achieved the right basis for a good relationship?*

Magali: When the time comes that a

horse reacts to a given event in the way you have trained him and not as he would have done at the start of your work together. You observe this in simple daily events such as when you let him loose in the paddock and he goes off quietly, or when he shows no fear at being given a bath and enjoys the rub down. At some point, you'll see that he has accepted your rules of behavior and he feels secure for having done so. Each day he demonstrates that he has accepted you as his leader, not as an authoritarian but a leader who reassures him. I always let a horse have his say and only curb it when he goes too far down the wrong road. I want him to see the problem, listen to my instructions, but work out how he will react. This can be very important in everyday life, but especially for our horses being constantly exposed to new situations when we are away performing our shows.

The second phase of what you might call "reconstruction" is equally important. This is when you begin to ride the horse and make more complex demands. Confidence and respect are no longer enough; the horse has to make an effort to learn to work with you. On

the whole, horses are cooperative because they want to learn and to please you. But beware! Every horse has his own rhythm and his limits, both physical and psychological, and you must know and respect them.

Agnès: *Besides mutual trust, what conditions are needed in order to further the training?*

Magali: In order to work effectively with a horse once you start riding him, besides mutual confidence you need to establish a framework that the horse understands. Up to the age of seven or eight the emphasis is on building the right muscles and suppleness. You need to get across to the horse what you require from him and to give him the means of delivering it. When he understands this he will understand what he is aiming for and will know when things are going correctly. Then the exercise becomes simple for him. You need a lot of patience and sometimes you have to abandon what you had planned for the day in order to return to an earlier stage of the program. Some trainers do the oppo-

site of this: they press on regardless, sometimes repeating a stage for an hour or more until the horse gives way. This is hardly the best method of keeping the horse happy about his work.

In more complex work, there will be times when you do have to push him a little but once I see in his eyes that he is losing his confidence, I never insist. What I might do is change what we are doing together and give him a good rub down or a massage. I know I must get it across to him that I wish him no harm and that everything is fine between us.

Agnès: *Even so, you have deadlines to keep, in the context of your shows. How do you cope with these?*

Magali: Losing the trust of a horse would be a much greater loss of time than not completing a couple of stages as planned. It doesn't matter a bit if a horse is not quite ready for his part in a show. I can always find something that will allow him to contribute with pleasure, however simple. I prefer to

swallow my pride in front of an audience rather than force the horse to do something he's not quite ready for and risk him losing his confidence and enthusiasm. I remember, when I was younger making this very mistake with Dao, pushing him too hard, and I can still recall the look he gave me. It makes me cringe with shame. Older and wiser, and because our shows are not so regimented as they once were, I go with the horse and his mood. This can apply to an experienced horse or one in training. He can be having an off day just like any athlete, so why should I force him to do something against his will and risk losing his enthusiasm?

Agnès: *How do you tend the balance between asking too much or too little of the horse?*

Magali: It's a question of choosing the right moment. Occasionally, we have to be firm and other times, let it go. We have to negotiate with our mature horses especially in mounted work. When, for instance, the energy level is low, I don't press ahead. We just do some simple exercises together and have a shorter session. If he's in fine fettle and understands what is wanted of him, I will be more demanding. I'm always gentle but I can be firm. On occasion, I will break off for a short interlude before returning to the exercise. I can also overcome any resistance by repeating the exercise during a walk in the countryside when we are all more relaxed. The desire to do well and a high energy level are the qualities I look for. I always prefer to be modest in my demands to avoid the work becoming onerous and demoralizing. This applies, in particular, to young horses that are not fully trained. In the case of stallions, it is a particularly delicate juggling act between remaining inflexible and negotiating a solution because they are always putting their relationship with the leader/trainer to the test.

Often, there are many changes taking place in the barn: some new arrivals and others leaving for our training center in Tarascon. This tends to raise the level of tension so I have to remind the stallions, sometimes quite forcibly, of the rules of behavior: telling them where the limits lie has a calming ef-

fect. By doing so I reduce the tension before it gets out of hand.

Frédéric: The inexperienced rider often finds it difficult to understand what the horse is trying to communicate and, therefore, cannot react in the correct way. This rider might have difficulty in getting across to the horse what he wants, or the horse becomes tired and bored with having to repeat an exercise too often. He might demonstrate this by moving his tail in an agitated way or grinding his teeth. When riders do not notice these warning signs they tend to think it is some sort of personal affront ("The horse isn't paying any attention to me") and allow themselves to get angry ("I'm going to show you who is master here"). In fact, riders should, at this point, be stopping the exercise.

Being aware and watchful for a horse's "signals" is necessary not only while working him but also in the barn. If a horse is showing signs of stress in his stall, maybe we have asked too much of him, or asked him in the wrong way. Or, let's say a horse seems in a bad mood and doesn't turn his head to greet you, well, perhaps he is feeling

depressed or even ill. Should we move him to another stall? It is always up to us to read the signals that the horse is putting out all the time and understand what is going on.

You often hear people saying that a horse is stupid because he won't do this or that to order, and that he needs to be shown who is boss. To my mind, this is the wrong approach: his behavior is telling us that there is something wrong. We have to understand what it is and when we do, it makes for a viable relationship. How can we possibly think we have a good relationship with a horse if we cannot "listen" to him or notice when he is depressed or anxious? When a person is unwell he can try to explain it in words; a horse tries to tell you with all sorts of body language because he cannot not speak. It is up to us to learn how to "read" him.

Agnès: *In order to have a lasting relationship with a horse, do you have to be on the lookout all the time?*

Frédéric: The answer has to be yes!

Frédéric with Phoebus (previous page) and with Phoebus and Paulus (above).

It is all too easy to slip into habits, especially with a horse you know very well, so while working together you are only half concentrating on what you are doing—almost like on "autopilot." So, there is a real danger in always working with the same horse. I know I concentrate more when I work with a horse that I know less well: I am fully awake and aware of the signals he is giving me. I set fair rules of behavior and carefully regulate the amount of authority I use.

With my own horses, particularly my favorites, the rules are more confused. Good intentions are sometimes blurred by events. For instance, I have a very close bond with Fasto and I'm afraid to say he is the worst educated! I occasionally let Phoebus push me about a little. In a way it strengthens our bond but there is also a loss. Worse still, it makes me smile. I think that with these two horses I give more weight to the magic, intuitive element of our relationship rather than that of the trainer. The ideal relationship is somewhere between the two and is perhaps best described by our friend Linda Tellington-Jones, "Always stay positive. Always be ready to "listen." Be patient,

precise, and fair in what you ask; it makes no difference if it's a horse that annoys you, one to whom you are indifferent, or one to whom you feel drawn. What a task!

Agnès: When do you feel completely at one with your horse? What is the ideal relationship?

Magali: For us theatrical show people, it is essential that when we step into the arena with a horse that we can play with each other and improvise without a worry. To reach this state there has to be a bond that allows for one of the pair to suggest something and for the other to react appropriately. And it has to happen with deep respect and, above all else, with joy. At that point all the years of work and patience find their reward. Fortunately, this ideal state can last a long time. Bandolero and Dao both reached it at about seven to eight years old and went on taking part in shows until they reached 20.

Agnès: And so we must touch on the

last phase of a relationship, and tonally on death.

Magali: Old age happens. We become aware that a horse has less appetite for work. It is as if the light is dimming. But it is never a straight descent. It can stretch over many months or even years if the horse has no major health problems. Anyway, these can be alleviated by maintaining good muscle tone and suppleness of limbs. Sensible dressage work will achieve this but I never overdo it: the horse should be allowed to slow down gracefully. Then, one day, he will tell us that he no longer wants to work.

Templado suddenly made it quite clear to both of us that he wanted to go home. Other horses want to have no more demands made of them so we put them out in a field with their friends but that does not mean in a distant field! They are brought in every evening with the others and groomed as usual. We occasionally ride them and even do a few of the old routines for a laugh if they show any inclination. At first, they can feel a bit left out of things but gradually they acclimatize and make a new life. We watch them deteriorate physically quite quickly because they were so fit and strong before the retirement. There is also a psychological change as they slow down, withdraw into themselves, and even become a little tetchy when their new habits are interfered with— just like people! This is when I abandon all the old rules and let them do what they want: They wander about the stable yard irritating the other horses, crop the grass on our lawn, amble up to our table, nosing about and upsetting things, or they wander off to see the chickens and roll in the sand of the riding ring if it has been left open. They lead self-sufficient lives and their connection to humans is a little less strong than when they were at the height of their powers and working each day. But in this final chapter of their lives we make a point of listening to them and keeping them contented.

Frédéric: That is the key to our relations with the horses. We are more concerned that they are happy rather than that they are obeying our wishes. In this way they give of their best so it is to our advantage. We try to respond to their needs as they respond to ours, especially during performances. I always invite the horse to do what he wants and what gives him pleasure. When we are together in a ring I observe his habits (having a roll over there, nibbling my tie, or climbing onto something) and I try to invent an act that grows out of what I see. In this way, I go along with a horse's character and his particular skills. Whether at home or performing, my horses are always joyful and, in the end, it is this quality that the public responds to rather than a perfect performance in which the horse is lashing his tail and grinding his teeth, leading often to aggressive behavior toward his trainer. Building a proper relationship means one that applies to both of us, each with our own abilities and wishes. All too often dressage comes to mean the horse being used to satisfy only the human's wishes and this can be true however perfect the performance appears to be.

Keyword:
PATIENCE

For Magali and me the notion of allowing enough time is closely allied to that of patience. We had to learn how to wait as well as to control our emotions. It seems these days that such an idea is becoming ever more anachronistic. Everyone wants instant results but horses have their own rhythm, closer to nature, and at variance with any ideas involving deadlines, profitability, or even over-enthusiastic pressure toward some goal. Whether it concerns a horse being prepared for a show, or someone who has invested in a Grand Prix horse, or just an amateur rider with one hour per week to spare, there is only one rhythm to work to and that belongs to the horse. For anyone in a hurry, riding is not the right occupation. When a person is stressed, the horse can see it and soon becomes stressed himself. This leads to badly thought-out instructions on the part of the rider and a refusal to cooperate on the part of the horse. Impatience leads to conflict and things are worse when the two meet the next time. Soon horse and rider are in a spiral of frustration.

It should be exactly the opposite: the less time there is available the more patient you must be and the more you must listen. Again and again, I have noticed that the less stressed I am, the quicker I get the result I want. Even when there is an important deadline like the first night of a show in which millions of dollars have been invested, I make myself one hundred percent available to the horse, calm and attentive to his reactions and his rhythm. The more he is at ease and relaxed, the sooner he will provide what I am asking of him. Above all else, I try to make him comfortable,

and being at ease myself is an essential ingredient. Then I take the time to go through each step of the training in the right sequence, not missing anything out. The more I take care to explain each step, the quicker he can integrate the whole procedure and perform effectively. This does not mean endlessly repeating an exercise; if it is not learned quickly then it has not been properly understood and I must find another way to introduce it, and to teach him. This is the human's responsibility, not the horse's.

Some people buy expensive competition horses and plan a detailed training schedule to achieve their desired aim. When the horse does not fulfil their expectations, it is not because he's stupid but because the training plan doesn't suit him. In this case, it is best to find another way but all too often, the horse's character is blamed and so it is that brilliant horses appear on the competition scene and then disappear equally fast, all because the rider has not been prepared to adapt his methods. It is often better to lower the bar of expectation for a time. I find if I press forward too quickly the horse will not reach his potential. The only solution is to go back a few steps and repeat those that have been rushed or missed out.

You never lose time by taking more time, and particularly by taking time to enjoy the horse's company. Make him as happy as yourself and you will progress at the right speed!

Frédéric Pignon

Communication is a key word. Without it we can never build a proper relationship with any horse. In reality, our two species are so different that it is not easy to transmit our own thoughts nor to receive the horse's. In order to get started in understanding his, first we have to acquire knowledge about his fundamental needs as a horse. This requires a study of animal behavior as well as the ways in which horses communicate between themselves. Theoretical knowledge of the subject will get you going, but you have to learn to watch so closely that you pick up the smallest signal: Why is that ear moving differently than usual? Why is there tension in his face or in his body? You can try putting yourself in his place. Then ask yourself: How would I react at this moment and in this place to the question you have just asked him or the request made? If I were feeling stressed or not too well, how would I react? Would I like the way demands were being made of me?

Ethologists hold up their hands in horror at the concept of anthropomorphism but I am convinced that one has to put yourself into the horse's skin if you are to gain an understanding. This does not mean that you can assume the horse will react to every situation similarly to a human reaction. It is a more a matter of being aware of the difficulties the horse experiences in communicating with a human and sometimes of the conflicting demands made upon him. A person may decide that the horse is paying no attention to her and that he is doing this as some sort of revenge. But revenge is not a weapon that a horse has in his armory. When things go wrong he can feel grief or lack of understanding and a sensation of tiredness, but there is no thought of revenge or harming the human.

What is evident and causes problems is that a horse has a developed sense of fairness and justice. We have to be fair in the analysis of a situation and in our actions that result from this. Some horses will rebel against what they perceive as unjust. They notice immediately if their own signals have not been received and decoded, but react wonderfully when they know have. Once they have confidence in us they can be a proper partner. It is not a matter of giving into their wishes but of acting justly and taking into account their interests, their comfort, and indeed ours at the same time!

In their world communication is not seeded with difficulty though some horses might appear a little withdrawn while others are the opposite. It is the same when they communicate with people, but even a quiet or withdrawn horse will start communicating once he sees that a person is inviting dialog. It is up to us to make the opening moves and I guarantee the horse will soon become a chatterbox.

Frédéric Pignon

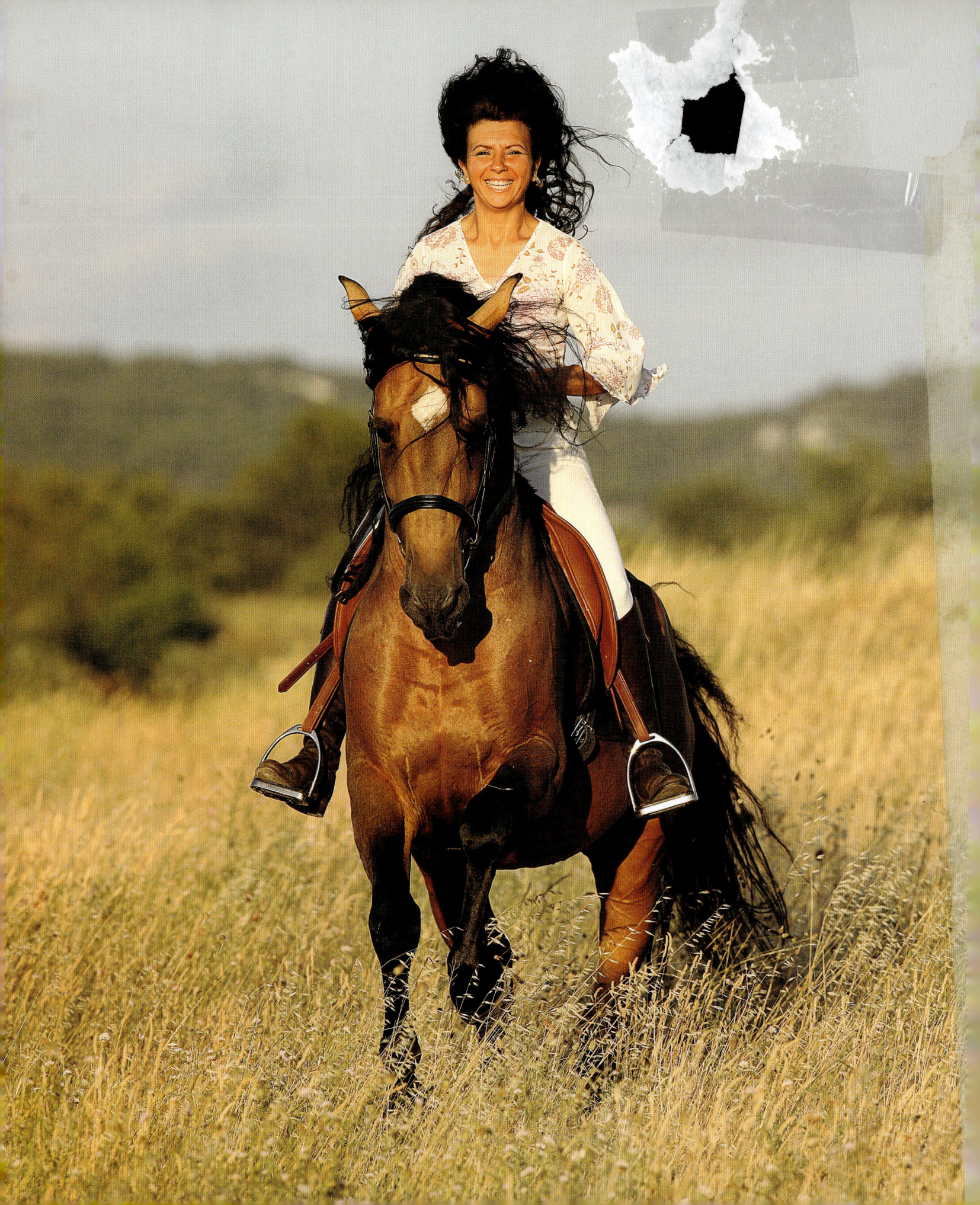

Letter to
Mandarin

When you were born I had already been dreaming of a golden brown horse for years. Then, one day, I saw the horse of my dreams. "That's the one for me!" I told my parents. "I shall call him Mandarin." Of course, I had no idea at that moment what lay ahead for the two of us but I was very taken with you. Until you reached the age of two I left you in the herd. Then we began to work on steps toward the goal of competition. I soon saw that your talents needed a lot of patience and ingenuity to bring them to the surface.

Brilliant at the outset, I knew you were holding something back and could do even better. To achieve this, I went through stages that many riders would think ridiculous. You were peculiarly sensitive around the neck and back so that I had to change your saddle as often as three times a week. You would always make a little telltale sound when you felt the tension getting the better of you in these areas. I would massage you, adjust my riding position, always be on the look-out for the best rhythm, and limit the amount of work to suit you. I listened to you every moment we were together and you became an exceptional horse.

For the past 10 years you have been the tops in your field. Every year you have enabled me to reach a higher level of understanding of how you, as a horse, function. Thanks to you I have steadily refined the logic of my solutions in order to allow you to give of your best, which turned out to be a world-beating standard. Other horses have been great but none have looked after me as you have. None has taught me the absolute necessity of the lightest imaginable touch that allowed us to say, Now we can really ride. I feel, at last, that I have reached your level and we have achieved the perfect partnership and mutual affection that I dreamed of when I first saw you. Thanks to helping you to achieve your maximum, I have made progress toward mine.

Magali

Like perhaps no other couple, Frédéric and Magali have made their lives a perfect partnership with their horses. For them it is not work; they both feel it is a privilege to be doing what they like best whether going for an evening ride in the countryside near their stables with Mandarin and Guizo, or performing at a show.

They laugh and rejoice together over their successes and embrace when they are sad. Their love for one another and for their horses is one.

In the Pignon-Delgado family, the horses are integrated with every moment that passes. Morning or evening, their needs come first and the days unfold at their rhythm. Sometimes they wander into the garden to graze, or they might invite themselves to lunch and lay their heads expectantly on the tabletop. If they ever feel anxious in their stalls they call out for Magali and Frédéric to come and share their unease.

Recently, there has been an important addition to the family: a two-legged little animal, a boy by the name of Noah. When he has trouble sleeping Magali sets off across the fields with her pet crow on her shoulder, singing songs to him. Wandering along beside them is her old friend Bandolero, now the patriarch of the herd, who due to his age enjoys absolute freedom to go anywhere he chooses. Occasionally, he lays his head on Magali's shoulder or peers into the stroller but, by then, Noah is fast asleep. Only the crow objects to this idyll, fluttering about, cawing loudly, trying to persuade Bandolero to move off.

Frédéric watches from a distance and his expression betrays his contentment.

CHAPTER 3
Growing Up Together

"The horse shows us the way
            to wisdom but we have to
want to follow him."

Frédéric Pignon

48

Above: With Bandolero.

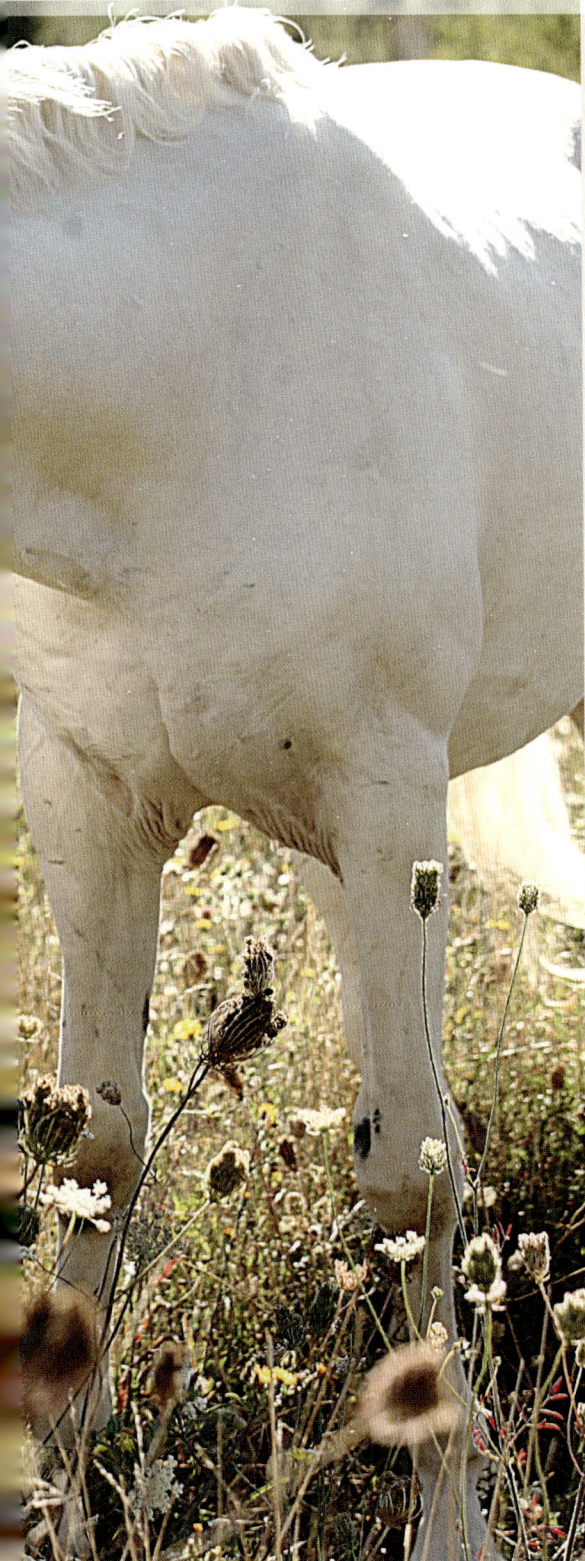

Agnès: Magali, don't you find that Bandolero seems just like a member of your family walking along beside you like that?

Magali: But he is a member of the family! He can do whatever he likes and when he comes close to the stroller I can read him so well I know it's safe. This scene seems perfectly natural to us. We want the horses to be happy, to develop their spirit of independence, their initiative, and their affection for us. How could I possibly tell him not to follow so closely when intimacy is what we have encouraged? The horses have taught us to take things as they come and be cool.

Agnès: In fact is it the horses that have been your teachers?

Magali: Of course! They have changed us utterly. When I was young, I was rather a tetchy, brittle character; they've taught me to be calm, to stand back and think before I act, to adapt to the circumstances and to be patient. Much more, I accept things as they are and try not to make everything turn out the way I had planned. Every day the horses teach us something. They make us adapt and really we have no choice because this is what keeps them happy and working well. If you cannot control your emotions and learn to listen, you will never get on well with a horse. And once you have won his trust, you do not want to ruin everything by allowing yourself a temper tantrum. No, you learn to control your reactions and to get around problems rather than face them head on. You can come back and deal with most things later.

Agnès: Have the lessons you have learned affected your relationships with people?

Magali: Yes, more than you can imagine. I was always quick to fire up as a girl and even to say unkind things. Now I listen, I reflect, I get rid of my emotions and then I calmly explain what I think. I take people as they are and I've also learned to look at them with empathy and understanding, whoever they are, as I do with the horses. I find now that I get an idea of someone's true nature very quickly. I think I can see quite clearly what they are after.

It is indeed horses that have taught us to accept life as it comes, with its highs and lows, and to be patient. We've kept hold of our aims but we travel the route to reach them with less stress and without inflexible goals.

But I never forget the need for absolute rigor. We must not take stupid risks: especially since most of our horses are stallions that are always pushing the limits to see how far they can go. So, there is a balance between insistence and being patient, between rigor and openness. Some people believe that we have lost a bit of an edge in the horses' performance by having such respectful and affectionate

Above: With Guizo and Mandarin.

relations with them. There are those that deliberately maintain barriers between themselves and their horses in order to keep them performing in the way they want. But how do you define "performing"? Some think that what we do is all a waste of time. They don't dare lose their control over these noble and powerful animals, so they subjugate them without mercy.

Frédéric: You cannot assume that contact with horses automatically improves your personality. If someone wants to improve he can do so with or without the help of a horse, but I am convinced that contact with a horse can help the process by teaching patience, the need to listen and observe, self-control and empathy. In some way, this contact helps us on the road to wisdom. But you still have to have the desire to set out on the journey! Those who do not follow this road can sometimes use the horse so they can become more authoritarian and pretentious. In our horse world, I come across beautiful people and those who have "dried up": they no longer question anything they do nor have any joy in it. The onerous demands of running a large stable as well as the isolation

that this dedicated life can lead to exhausts their curiosity. They can no longer see the horses with fresh eyes. I myself find there are periods when I am more or less in tune but when it comes to the horses, I have the same intense devotion that I had when I set out. I was really antisocial as a youngster and it was horses that taught me to learn to love people just as I have always tried to love any horse that I work with, even those that do not

attract me. I've learned to look for the positive aspects of someone's character and to credit progress rather than concentrate on the areas of disagreement. I've learned to accept people as they are.

Agnès: *Does a horse also change character as a result of human contact?*

Magali: If a horse is happy and loved in the right sense of the term, he opens up and shows his true character. His eyes will sparkle and he'll communicate all the time, expressing his desires and showing affection. Of course, some horses respond faster than others and if a horse is by nature very timid, you have to let him know that he has the right to express his true feelings. Some could be said to change character completely. I remember how crazy and scowling Mandarin was at the outset, whereas now he is full of enthusiasm as well as being tender and extroverted.

By contrast, a horse that has been kept down and not allowed to blossom becomes indifferent or aggressive. The light has gone out. While mounted you may get him to do whatever you want but once you dismount he only thinks of fleeing. Horses that are understood become more self-sufficient, creative, and courageous. Horse and human can unquestionably influence each other but a horse is not automatically improved by contact with a person, only by a good relationship with him.

Frédéric: There is no doubt in my mind that a person can influence a horse either for good or for ill. Horses are, by nature, prey animals and, therefore, fearful of the unknown. If a man can, by his fair-minded authority and ability to listen, liberate the horse from this fear, he has chased away the horse's principal enemy. Once liberated, the horse is capable of sizing up any situation and deciding how to act. Leaders are the ones that learn to control their stress; those that don't, follow. Learning to control his fears is the best gift a horse can receive, and when he achieves this state in partnership with a human, the resulting bond is strong.

Agnès: *Have you ever been disappointed by a horse?*

Frédéric: No! It is only when you build expectations in return for all the work you have invested in a horse that it can lead to disappointment. You have to remember a horse is always a horse and can only reward you with what is in his "horse nature." If you can become one of the horse's priorities, that is already a huge achievement. Disappointment arises from using human values in your expectations: a "fair return" is not a concept to embrace. What counts is the relationship you build, the things you learn from it, and the ways in which it makes you a better person. Benefit from your time together without imagining that the horse can change in an anthropomorphic way into something else! By deriving and giving pleasure, you evolve in a good way and become more positive. A good relationship helps you to grow and the horse to flourish but you are still profoundly different creatures. That is what makes the adventure worthwhile and full of fascination.

Keyword:
OPENNESS

For the horse and our relationship to come in a good way, we have to remain open. In my imagination, I see open doors between us so that we always feel that physically and mentally we can achieve anything we set our minds to. If we rest on the principles we have been taught or learned, the relationship with the horse will stay shuttered. Every day I try to make a fresh start: this is a new day for me and for this horse I am with. What will happen? If I do not take this approach—and there are plenty of people in the horse world who do not—I shall never really get through to this horse and learn about his true nature.

With the passage of time and all the experiences we have had, both good and bad, Magali and I have become not exactly fatalistic but aware of how limited the possibilities are of influencing the course of life. I would say that we have become excited and amused by the thought of all the unexpected things that happen. Long ago, we gave up wanting to control everything and, in fact, we listen more and more to what the horses tell us they want to do. For instance, I chose Dao as one of my circus act horses but he became Magali's number-one dressage horse. I don't know how it happened; there was never any hard and fast decision: we let it happen. To me, being open means being in tune with myself and others, not having immutable principles but always having the wish to be as fair as possible. For the horse to have a beneficial effect on us we must remain open. We must entertain a sense almost of abandon so that we are always ready to be surprised and moved, and ready to question all our previous experience in order to find the true way forward.

Frédéric Pignon

You might think that because we stress the importance of the horse being relaxed and also because he is often working freely, that we are not rigorous in our methods. On the contrary, we train stallions to have a lot of ideas for themselves and enjoy a large degree of freedom of action. For this reason, we have to remain in control of the situation the whole time and be aware of the slightest sign of conflict or any infraction of the rules we set. From the very moment we go into a stall with a horse, for example, to groom or unsaddle him before he is released into a paddock, we concentrate 100 percent on every movement he makes, on his facial expressions, and his body language. It is only because of this that he listens to us, respects us, and tries to do what we ask of him rather than taking an interest in the other horses and risk walking over our feet.

Naturally, it demands rigor because it requires uninterrupted concentration, not easy to keep up for a whole day. For Fred and me, it is second nature, as if a part of our brains were like that of a horse, always on the lookout and interacting with the rest of the herd. This rigor reassures the horses in two ways: They know they are being listened to by the human in the same way as they are by their equine mates, and, what is more, that the human will guide and protect them. They feel in a position to relax and be confident. They know what is expected of them and what their position is, exactly as in their own social life in the herd. Surprisingly perhaps, the rules of the herd are also extremely rigorous where no divergence is permitted. Even as foals, they must obey the rules of the herd and of the individual horses. In the course of our work with

them this rigor must be obtained without a break, whether it is with foals "in hand" or during the most complex mounted procedures. All through the series of exercises, I know at each stage what I aim to achieve, and I give the horses framework so they can also feel they are making progress.

Everything I have said applies more to the stallions than to any other horses because they are the quickest to become excited. They always nibble away at authority in order to be top of the pecking order, which is not always a good scheme. These highly sensitive creatures are easily led astray by their emotions and soon reach the point where they lose control. If they get to this state, they take risks that are a danger both to themselves and those around them. It is, therefore, important to give them a clear framework that is not, however, imposed with military strictness, but with loving firmness so that they calm down. You can amuse yourself with them but you must always be careful not to lose their attention. You must recognize the smallest signals and respond to them just as would happen in the herd.

When I have students, I notice that it is not easy to get across the necessity of maintaining this rigor 100 percent of the time. But for us who are there all the time and live with horses, it gives a great feeling of well-being. It enables us to distance ourselves from everyday worries. With the horses we can be quite simply ourselves, without any pretensions. We can "let go" and this renews the inner strength that we need to face a new day.

Magali Delgado

Letter to

Dao

This account is almost too wonderful to be true. You changed my life for good: Your character and your determination showed me the path to a new way of working. You allowed me my mistakes, you put up with my excesses. You taught me how to speak with you, and always with gentleness. Your patience was the basis of my knowledge. No wonder I thought of you as "Master."

For a long time now, I have loved you with a deep respect. Your look touched me to the core and I felt that your eyes mirrored our relationship. I wanted you to be happy.

What a great partnership we were! Every competition or show was for me unforgettable: an event to recall with pleasure. And then there were those special times when the two of us, without bridle or saddle, galloped through the meadows, my hair and your mane flying in the wind. Who made the decision to stop or turn? Had we become a centaur? I have no idea. These were magic times and I don't know who the magician was.

Thank you, Dao! Few riders can have had the chance of such an intense, simple, honest, and beautiful relationship with their horse.

Your hooves have marked my life just as they have the soil in the meadows. The sound they made will be forever with me.

Magali

Magali's smile, as she presses her cheek to Dao's, gives an idea of her joy when she is close to him. They are simply relishing a light-hearted moment. Magali knows in her heart that Dao would never do anything to harm her. The trust is absolute. What a bond and what love between the two of them and all without the ability to communicate in words.

Without a doubt, Templado was the most important horse in Frédéric's life. When I first met Frédéric he told me about his relationship with the horse, and the horse's death after a long illness. I could sense the sadness mixed with love and gratitude. It was clear that he still felt the loss as keenly as ever.

Gabriele knew of his feelings only too well and she was nervous about how he might react to her present: a large print on linen of Frédéric and Templado running through a summer meadow, shoulder to shoulder, the horse's mane mingling with Fred's long hair, as happy as two children. Time seemed to have stood still.

When Gabriele unrolled the picture in front of him, I saw his eyes darken and could sense the turmoil in his heart. For a few moments he was speechless, then he thanked Gabriele, turned around and went off to be with his horses.

In spite of the pain of this experience, I felt I needed to explore with both Frédéric and Magali the subject of loss and how they coped with it.

CHAPTER 4

Losing and Finding Yourself Again

"The horse distances himself
from you and cuts himself off
because he knows that now you
cannot help him."

Frédéric Pignon

A light mist hung over the meadow; the grass was still heavy with dew. Templado was celebrating his freedom together with Frédéric, his friend, racing side by side through the wet grass. Two beings with the same heartbeat. A moment never to be recaptured.

Today it is only a memory but what has never changed is the feeling of profound happiness this moment engendered. Frédéric only has to close his eyes to recapture "that first fine careless rapture." Templado is still ever present in his heart.

Magali Delgado & Frédéric Pignon

Above: With Templado.

Agnès: *Are you still devastated when you see a photo of Templado?*

Frédéric: For ages I could not come to terms with it. If he had not been ill for so long and had I not been with him when he died, it would have been even worse.

Now, with the passage of time and greater maturity, I have been able to. I have accepted that life continues and that no one can take away or diminish this amazing relationship we had together. I was profoundly affected by his death but I pulled myself together again, and now I know what risks I run in becoming so attached to a horse. When I was young I had no idea. I acknowledge that each new relationship is unique, irreplaceable, magical, and that death is part of the bargain. This acceptance gives even more weight and importance to each relationship. Since Templado, I value each horse, every moment I spend with him, and

every new level that we reach. With 40 horses, there are a lot of deaths awaiting us but nowadays we cope with it differently. In a way, we have tamed it because we know what to do, namely to be with the horse to the last moment of his life, making sure that the conditions are as comfortable for him as they can be. We grieve, of course, but we are at peace. This is how we coped with Dao's death, Dao who had been with Magali for more than 20 years.

Agnès: *Magali, tell me about Dao's death if you can.*

Magali: What was important to me above everything else was that he should not feel abandoned, but happy and pampered through his illness, right to the last moment. I made sure there was someone with him when we were not able to be. I visited him many times each day and always tried to cheer him up. For the last four years, I daily fed him a kilo of carrots; I allowed him the

freedom of the stables so that he could talk to the other horses; he had the freedom of our garden: we went for walks every day and we would search out the tastiest herbs for him to chew. Although I never made much fuss of another horse in the barn because he always had his eye on me, these were special, private moments between the two of us. Apart from that, I groomed him for as long as I could spare and tried to compress disagreeable actions, like giving him medications, to the shortest time I could.

When, later on, he began to get weaker, I put myself entirely at his disposal and since the "Master" knew what he wanted, it was easy. During the last few weeks of his life I lived every day as though it were his last. It was tough but a profound experience. On his last evening I left him longer than usual in the garden and went to see him after dinner. He was lying down, obviously not well, but calm. I told him how much I thanked him for all that he had done for me and recalled all our triumphs together. When I saw that he was quite tranquil, even though covered in perspiration, I went to bed but was soon up again to see him. When I reached his stall I saw that he was dead. He appeared to be at peace.

How I miss him but I feel I did everything I could to ease his last moments. And the manner of his passing was in character: dignified, calm, and without fuss. A classy horse to the last! It was such a relief to me that his end was in this manner and not as sometimes, involving violence, sickness, and finally euthanasia. Horses often die quite suddenly so you have to be prepared psychologically, though however well prepared you are, it is always a terrible shock.

What brings comfort to me is that I was with Dao right to the end. If I had been away at his passing, I would forever have felt guilty and miserable.

Agnès: *Are you not tempted occasionally to project a relationship, lost through death, onto a new horse?*

Magali: You should not, but since Dao went, I am hoping for a new, important relationship with one of his sons who has much in common with his father, both mentally and physically. I hear myself telling him this, but at the same time, I know what I'm about. I know my relationship will be uniquely with him, even if occasionally he reminds me of his father and I allow myself a moment of nostalgia.

Frédéric: As Magali says, every relationship is unique. It is built up of a thousand little exchanges, incidents lived through together, shared moments that result in a connection that cannot be reproduced. Our aim is to treat every horse as an individual in his own right, not to overlook his special qualities that belong to no one else, and not to expect him to put on the hide of another horse.

Agnès: *Once you have established a good relationship, is it possible to lose it even though you are riding the horse every day?*

Frédéric: It is indeed possible when

you forget the rules of a proper relationship. If you just care for him as you have been used to, and ride him as you normally do but without looking at your actions afresh, without excitement about what you are going to do today, the relationship will start to fade and may even be extinguished—as with people. As in the lives of every couple, you must remain inventive and creative. Every day I see people who no longer know what to do with their horses. They simply repeat what they have done before and do not make any attempt to try something new. It is not easy for any of us to avoid this from time to time. Once things become automatic, boredom sets in and then the relationship goes to sleep.

When I was performing every day in *Cavalia*, riding the same horse at the same time each day, I, myself, let things slip. I noticed that occasionally I passed in front of a stall without taking the time to greet a horse because I reckoned I would be seeing him that evening in the show. This led me to feel, after a year had passed, that I was cutting myself off from the horses even though I was performing with them each day. When the realization

Above, right, and following page: Lancelot.

hit me, I found it impossible to bear. I told myself that I was living a lie, presenting a relationship during a performance that in reality no longer existed. I felt as though I had made a pact with the Devil in order to assure the continuity and success of the show and in so doing, had lost everything that was dear to me: a unique, powerful, intuitive, and respectful relationship with each horse. My work was still professional but the heart had gone out of it. I was so frightened when I acknowledged this to myself that I almost gave up. Then I realized that the solution lay not by running away but by doing things differently.

I appealed to the people I most respected like Linda Tellington-Jones. The journey was long and arduous because it is more difficult to reinvent a relationship than to build one for the first time. I had to abandon my old habits and my way of thinking. I had to question everything I did. Finally, I found the way to perform each evening without putting my relationships with the horses in danger: I had to allow them a much greater degree of liberty and give them the chance of suggesting what we did at any moment. This appealed to their creativity and to their excitement. It enriched the shows and allowed the horses to reach greater heights of achievement.

74

Every evening I had to adapt at an instant to whatever the horses decided to do, and not do what I had planned; in the end this crisis served us well. It enriched the lives and capabilities of the horses and, therefore, the shows; it taught me how to listen to the horses much more effectively than I had previously. I became more confident and calm. I now know that when a relationship has a wobbly moment, there is a solution.

Agnès: *How can one find a solution to avoiding boredom with daily routines?*

Frédéric: The easiest thing is to say, "It's not working so I'll give up." Or you could decide to let the relationship remain on a purely functional basis and accept that the quality of it is not the priority. For Magali and me, that would now be impossible. I had such an experience with my first horse and sold him. Now I would accept that it is I who would have to adapt and, thereby, find a solution to the problem. Templado was the best example of this dilemma. Nothing seemed to work: he was angry, difficult, even dangerous. I could easily have given up and sold him but I persevered in trying to understand what he was asking of me. When I did, he turned out to be an exceptional horse, the best one I shall ever have.

Nowadays, I favor the quality of a relationship over any technical achievement. Because I do not attempt to dominate the horse (often leaving him to show initiative) nor insist on details, my relationship is of an extraordinary intensity; there is no danger of it becoming rusty. Thanks to this, the horse and I have such pleasure in being together that the feeling comes across to the audiences watching our performances.

Agnès: What practical advice can you give to someone who feels the quality of a relationship diminishing?

Magali: If you have a really strong relationship with a horse, it stays that way but you have to be on the lookout all the time in case the horse is saying, "If you do this or that, I do not agree and I shall stop cooperating with you." When you notice the horse looking at

you out of the corner of his eye or you can tell he is not pleased to see you, or when he's grumpy or disinclined to obey you, it is because he is not happy. He's withdrawing because what you have on offer is not what he wants. Whenever this happens, it is always our fault in my experience and not the horse's. I am occasionally so busy and preoccupied that a horse will go into a sulk. It would be easy to treat this as one more worry but that is the wrong attitude. You have to realize that the

horse knows what you are doing and is inviting you to open up, start listening to him again, and renew your appetite for the relationship. Once he sees you responding he will be full of enthusiasm again. For instance, if I see Mandarin in a bad mood, I know I have to relax and go for a good ramble with him in the fields. The solution is never to say, "Things are not going well at the moment for me so I'll let the horse be until things improve." You simply cannot leave horses in their stalls for days on end so I spend say 20 minutes instead of the usual longer time, and without any preconceived idea of what we want to do, go for a short ride, or a walk, or just being together. If I force myself to ride without really wanting to, he knows, and nothing is achieved. Also, he will let me know! Better to have a shorter time together but make it quality time.

Agnès: *When a horse is no longer being worked, how do you keep up the relationship?*

Frédéric: When a horse retires it is best to make it a gradual process, and to build a new relationship in order to avoid letting the connection die when you stop the activities he has been used to doing. If he's no longer performing in shows then you have to find a new activity he will enjoy that is within his capabilities. It takes a few

Above: With Phoebus.

77

months of transition to make the horse accept that his position in the barn has undergone a change, but if you do it carefully and with understanding, he will soon settle down in his new capacity. You will find your horses stay happy in retirement.

Agnès: *Sometimes, it is us who cannot, either for professional or personal reasons,* give the same amount of time to our horse. In this case, how do we avoid breaking off the relationship?

Magali: It is better to spend a little good quality time with your horses than a lot of bad quality time. We have gone through this experience with our son, Noah. The moment he arrived we had to devote time and energy to this little chap, time and energy that we had previously lavished on the horses, but his presence gave us such joy that the whole barn was aware of it and benefited from it. We seem to have communicated the excitement of becoming parents to all those around us, that is, the horses. So, even though we could spend less time with them, everything was fine and they shared in our happiness.

Above, right, and following page: Mandarin.

Keyword:
RISK TAKING

The real danger in any relationship is to stop seeing rather than stop looking. People often allow themselves to be dulled by their habits. They always do the same thing and if you ask them about it they say that the horse cannot do something, for example: be in a field with other horses, cross a river, enter the trailer, or go out riding in a group. In reality, it is the person who raises the barrier to hide behind and avoid facing what he fears. He has arranged his activities to avoid taking any risk, even though he understands it is not an ideal solution. The result: the rider lacks confidence in himself and in his horse. To avoid setbacks he refuses to try anything new. But it is only by doing so and facing problems together that he will build a lively and enriching relationship with his horse. You do not have to take dangerous risks but you must always be on the lookout for new experiences that will broaden your ability.

Frédéric Pignon

Keyword:
ABANDONMENT

You often hear about old horses being abandoned alone all day in a field without any physical contact. But there is also psychological abandonment. This is what a horse feels when no one pays attention to him, looks at him, or shares anything with him. It can happen when we get a new horse; the old horse watches, tries to communicate, but our attention is elsewhere. There is a tendency to imagine that when a horse retires he should be content at not having to work so hard. "He's recovered the real horse's life," we might say to ourselves. In fact, it's not like that for him. He is used to a certain rhythm, he had his place in the barn, and in our lives. This is what made sense to him and then suddenly all is changed. We could give him the odd carrot and brush him down daily, thinking that is what an old horse needs. In reality, the best solution is not to project on him an image of peaceful retirement but to keep listening to him and see what makes him happy.

In Dao's case he liked being ridden regularly. Without being asked he would do a few piaffes and Spanish Steps while passing younger horses in order to show off. For another horse, it might be a massage or a game he craves. It will depend, too, on the mood of the horse. I watch people religiously brushing their horse each day for an hour, though I can see quite clearly that the horse is not in the mood for it. In the end, he doesn't want to see a human being let alone a brush, he's so fed up. You have to learn that there's a way between these extremes of making a horse happy but it depends entirely on listening to what pleases him. He is the only one who can tell you.

Magali Delgado

Letter to *Templado*

It was the evening we got back from Spain after two months of Cavalia shows. As always, you were waiting for us and I spent an hour with you, telling you how great it was that you were still holding on even though your health had been deteriorating steadily for some time. But on that evening, you did not appear to be too bad and you were clearly glad to see us. I felt anxious despite your good humor so I followed my instincts as always and went back after dinner to spend more time with you. Next morning I gave you a good wash down; I don't know why but I felt you had to be clean. You let me do it with patience even though you had long since gotten bored with showers. I called Magali to come and see how long your mane was now: it touched the ground. I let you out into the garden to graze and then visit your friends whom you enjoyed irritating a little. It made me smile, but underneath I knew…. The sun was climbing into the sky: it was going to be a hot July day. At midday a friend came to see me. It was as if I were waiting for a bus: was it coming or not? Doubtless he could feel my anxiety.

Sipping coffee in the house I had one eye on you as you grazed in the garden. Suddenly, you lay down. I knew the bus had come. I ran outside to get you up: it was not good for you to be lying down in that merciless sun. You obliged and followed me to your stall where you lay down again. A sense of panic continued to rise in my throat. I knew the moment I dreaded had now arrived. I admit that for a second or two I wished I were miles away but your calm restored my reason and I knew you needed me to be there.

We had to live this moment together: you to leave, and me to accept your going. I came near you. I felt your warmth as you began to breathe deeply. I laid my hand on your head as a mother would on her child's. You were perspiring and growing frailer by the minute. You tried to get up a few times perhaps to look out at the meadow where we had run and played together so often. You seemed to accept that it was time to leave and that there would be no returning. At the end you looked like a foal who had just been born and I was trying to tell myself that this was but life's cycle: the coming and the going. Your strength was failing. You made a little movement of your head and then you lay still.

A poem that Pierrot wrote at your birth came into my mind and it calmed me. I understood at a profound level that life goes on: this last page had turned and the great book of your life had shut. I felt that nothing would be the same again for me. We had drunk the nectar of life from the same cup. You taught me so much and now being with you at your death the experience had helped me to understand life at its most intense.

Templado, I feel your energy around me; it radiates from the walls, the ground, and the longeing ring where we lived so many intimate moments together. I think of how sometimes a little white butterfly would circle about our heads. Chiefly, I think of you, my beautiful white horse, I picture your mane flying in the wind, and I smile….

Frédéric

INSIGHTS

BY AGNÈS GALLETIER

When Gabriele Boiselle asked me to work with her on the book about Frédéric and Magali, she warned me that this would be a very special experience. She was right: in my 30 years of riding and 20 years as a riding correspondent, I have never come across this quality of relationship between horse and human. When I met Frédéric and Magali I knew that I had come face to face with a relationship I had only previously dreamed about, one in which it was possible to communicate to this degree. You only have to observe the couple at work with their horses in the stable to be aware of the quality of the contact: a playful, spontaneous understanding in which the horse is clearly drawn to the trainer, watches him and revels in it.

So often I saw horses approaching Frédéric in the longe ring, laying their soft noses on Frédéric's chest or his neck, or seeking out his hand to share the bodily contact and claim his attention.

It's possible that I didn't find these displays so unusual at first until one summer morning I saw Frédéric taking Phoebus and Paulus, the two Friesian stallions, to the fields by the barn. These two lively young creatures sprang out of their stalls, without halters, only to find themselves between the herd on one side of them in the paddock and grazing mares on the other. I could see that the temptation to go one way or the other was tremendous. They were bursting with energy, their nostrils flaring and their ears moving back and forth; their eyes sparkled and their hearts were visibly pounding under their shiny coats, but in spite of all this, they quietly followed Frédéric to carry out what he had asked them to do. That was more interesting than the temptations that surrounded them.

Magali stood next to me smiling with pride at the sight. This incident was for me a good introduction to the question of dominance and connection.

Previous page: Fasto and Aetes.

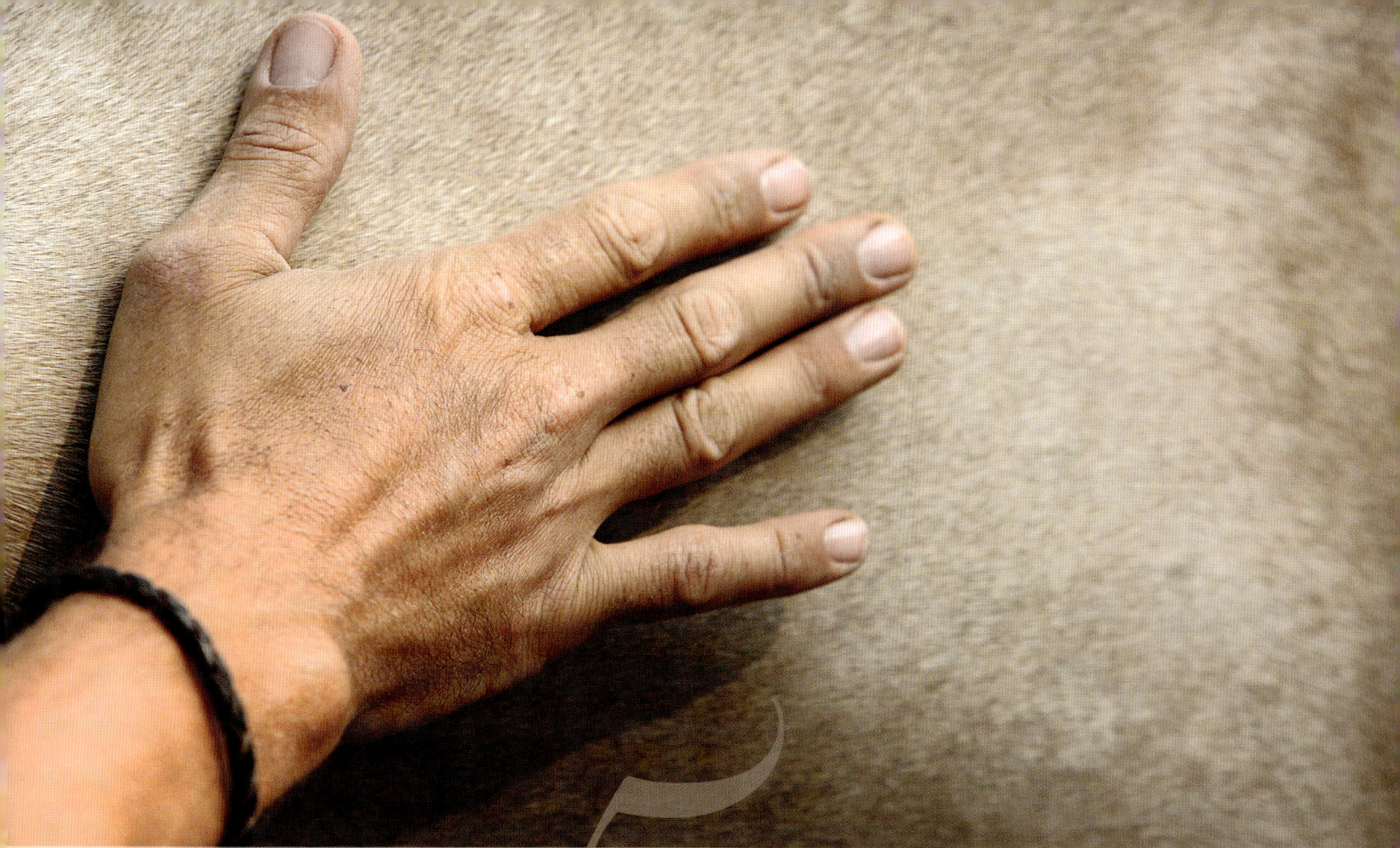

5

The Strength of the Connection

"When two thousand people are aware of the
positive energy and tenderness of our horses who
come freely and calmly toward us in order to be stroked,
then I feel I can talk about the incredible
resonating spirit that clothes the world."

Frédéric Pignon

Above: Nacarado.

Agnès: *Magali, how do you explain that your connection with the horses is so strong that you appear to be the focus of their lives and interests?*

Magali: When Frédéric is running beside his horses, there is a closeness equivalent to that between two people. It is a complete understanding between two male adults without the slightest untoward aspect. It's a game and as the human participant, Fred has to be careful. Given my size and limited endurance, it is not something I can take part in. Fortunately, the depth of this bond can express itself in other ways that bring me similar satisfaction. For instance, at our last shows together, Mandarin was puzzled by the spectators' applause; instead of galloping back to the exit after our performance, he returned to me in order to get my reassurance. In this way he showed me that he preferred to be re-assured by me rather than seeking the comfort of the other horses. I interpreted this as saying that our bond had become stronger than any other alternative, and that gave me great joy.

Agnès: *Frédéric, how do your relations with the horses affect you at the deepest level?*

Frédéric: I feel overwhelmed by the moments when I am totally in communion with them. I can even say that I feel as a horse does, namely in touch with my instincts, experiencing intuitive and swift reactions, in fact, like an animal. I sense that my brain is registering every detail that is happening, just as theirs is, even the tiniest signals that make up non-verbal communication. Without spending time on reflection, I find I am capable of deciding on the right action in any situation. I sense that I am returning to the freshness and innocence of my childhood.

Children take in what happens around them all the time, trying to understand, without being influenced by principles, education, or a concept of what is considered normal or acceptable behavior. As adults, our reactions are guided by what is considered appropriate given our education and cultural background. We no longer really look at things. Whatever happens to us, we see it through our life's experience and our response is conditioned by it.

When I am surrounded by my stallions, all tremendously powerful, hypersensitive creatures, boiling with energy, I haven't the time to analyze what is going on. My exchanges with them are visual, tactile, sensual, and even forceful on occasion. Only my instinct allows me to react in time to every situation. Later, I can analyze what happened and make a judgment about my reaction. This kind of experience forces me to abandon all my training and accepted ways of dealing with nation of freedom, combined with elegance and great strength that make the horse such a potent symbol and the subject of dreams. The duality of energy and fragility, elemental strength and sensitivity has given humans the desire to tame this beast, and to prove to themselves that they can master the animal and their fear of him because of his far greater strength.

However, there is another scenario, that of helping the horse to master his fears. At this stage, we have to find a way into his world in order to communicate with him and find solutions together. It is not similar to working with a dog or cat, fascinating as that can be. With a horse you have constantly to be prepared to question your experience and try to enter the world of the particular horse you are working with. Any dedicated rider will tell you that the struggle to learn is never over; a lifetime of devoted study is insufficient. For a human this journey, beset by pitfalls and questioning, is profoundly satisfying, because it keeps us on the go. It feeds our desire for self-improvement, and unlike with other animals, it affords us a sensual dimen-

situations; I have to learn new ways and that is immensely enriching, not only in dealing with animals but with humans.

Nowadays, in addition to my intellectual understanding, I have another more instinctive and intuitive understanding and the two are complimentary. Weighing up the pluses and minuses before deciding on a course of action simply does not work with horses; the experience of working with them means that I can take in a lot of information quickly and make up my mind on the spot. I'm not saying I'm always right but I know I can intuitively adapt very quickly, find solutions, know which direction to take in a way that I feel comfortable.

Agnès: *What is it that attracts humans to horses?*

Frédéric: I suppose it is the combi-

sion to our experience. This is perhaps to do with the size of the creature, his gentleness and warmth. We feel small and protected, at the same time as being carried along. We enter his world, share his bodily odors and noises; it is a physical intimacy with the feeling of being sucked into his bubble. You cannot have this feeling with smaller animals even when you are holding them in your arms.

Magali: I find that the horse allows us to have emotions that are at the same time strong, contradictory, and instantaneous. Most people are in some way attracted to horses but they are frightened of them. They are impressed by the horse's speed and strength, even their wildness, then touched by their gentleness and apparent fear. During our shows people laugh, hold their breath, cry, have goose bumps, all without knowing why. The horses produce a gamut of emotions that throw them from one extreme to the other. The adrenaline rush can become quite addictive!

Agnès: What is the most important thing that horses have given you?

94

Magali: Pure happiness. I think I live the happiest moments of my life with horses. After a good day with them, I am overflowing with so much positive energy I could move mountains. Ever since I was a child I felt I could not live without this feeling. It is the center of my life and everything else feels a little superfluous because it is time that could have been spent with the horses.

Fortunately, this link has not just been an ego trip for me. I used to be impatient and obstinate; horses have taught me to acknowledge another's existence and rhythm. I have learned to control my emotions and, from being a proud person, always sure of myself, I hope I have learned humility. Horses teach you not to go beyond certain limits because if you do so, you can undo months of work.

After all these years I am less impulsive; I now think before I give my opinion, and I acknowledge that there is always more than one solution to a problem, not only my own! I think the experience and joy that I have had living with horses has generally rounded my character and made the rough places, if not smooth then certainly a little smoother.

Frédéric: I have always been a bit of a dreamer so the horses nourish this side of my character. They satisfy my love of beauty but at the same time they keep me fully aware of the reality of the situation. Stallions are powerful creatures; you have to be on your guard all the time in order to avoid being crushed or knocked over, and on the lookout in case one of them jumps on another.

They have been my constant companions in my efforts to improve the way I communicate and to sharpen my reactions. I have always been intrigued by the calmness that radiates from Tibetan monks; I feel I have discovered the same secret through my life with horses. They have been my passport to being in communion with life and with others. They have given me the feeling that I am completely centered when I am working and that I can be open to others when I am not. Sometimes, when I am alone with horses in the show tent, I enter a state of total concentration, not unlike meditation, and it is, perhaps, the same as prayer. This relationship that is an unending succession of new questions and new answers feeds my thirst for spirituality, and fortifies my love of life.

Agnès: What are the reasons behind putting on your shows?

Magali: The shows enable us to share our work and our beliefs with the public. It is a spur to progress, as long as we are satisfied with the outcome! It is also a source of encouragement to the horses, who clearly love taking part. You should see the way they walk up into the trucks when we are setting off for a new show venue. They are excited by the prospect of new stables and, once they are performing, are bursting with pride and full of energy. An audience has the effect of making them even more enthusiastic than they are at home.

During the shows we no longer have the sense of working but of taking part in an adventure in which all our senses are at their most alert, and our energy at its maximum. It is almost as if we are under a spell, and sometimes, I find that a horse I have been working with for months is transformed into quite a different character. Under a spotlight and with the eyes of the public on them, the horses seem to blossom. For all I know, the same thing happens to me!

The applause and the involvement of the audience recharge our batteries and we all give our best. I love feeling that we have enabled people to enter our world and to get an inkling of our relationship with horses. It makes me feel needed but it will only work as long as we, and the horses, are all enjoying ourselves. Should the shows ever lose their spontaneity and joy, we will pack it in and go home.

Agnès: *What do you consider is the message you are trying to get across to the audience?*

Magali: Above everything else, re-

spect for horses. Then there is the pleasure that we and the horses and the audience can derive from riding. I happen to be in love with dressage and with demonstrating that you can reach top-level technique without stress. I want to show people that without the usual restraints of a bridle, only using a simple collar, I can ask for piaffes or a change of step.

Audiences often tell us that our horses look happy; this is what moves them and gives them the incentive to try a different approach with their own mounts. It has been repeatedly drummed into them that the horse has to be forced to submit to their will and even that it is a stupid creature. Suddenly, they understand there is another approach: they start observing their horse, taking account of his needs, acknowledging that he is another being that responds, adapts, and negotiates with them. So it is that I hope our shows help to introduce the public to a richer relationship with horses, one in which nature, the earth, and simple values are all bound up in one. It is the only way to achieve real happiness.

Agnès: *Do you think that the horse has a*

98

meaningful role in our modern world?

Frédéric: I believe the world is made up of positive and negative energy. The more we can develop and combine positive energy, the more hope we can have for the future of the planet. The horse is clearly a means of bringing positive energy to humans: you only have to see how he makes people happy, including children, the mentally handicapped, and the sick. I remember the case of a woman near the end of her life, confined to a wheelchair, who begged her children to bring her back to see our show again. She said it revived her will to live.

The beauty of the horse plays a part in all this but is not a sufficient explanation. There is something about the way in which this creature produces in us a burst of energy and vitality, a feeling of joy that exceeds the sum of his own beauty, strength, and speed. In my opinion, he reaches something absolutely fundamental in us and he is capable of giving us new energy, bringing us into a more harmonious

Above, right, and following page: Nacarado.

state with ourselves and with the world about us.

This is why Magali and I want to go on giving shows. When two thousand people are conscious of this burst of positive energy as well as the tenderness the horses express, when they relax and come up to us for a hug, I know it does something for us, for

them, and in an unquantifiable way, for the world. We have even had people say that one of our shows has changed their life. I don't want to exaggerate but I am convinced that what we achieve in our shows helps to open a door toward understanding and sharing. People have been able to look again at their relationship with their horse and to choose an approach that is less domi-

nated by conventional teaching, but more open and responsive to the needs of the other. They have begun to listen and to believe in the power of their intuition. From that point, maybe they will also learn to listen more to others and change their attitude to the world about them. If so, the power of the horse is indeed great and we want to do our part to further it!

Keyword:
SENSE

I often feel myself pulled between my intuition, an instant reaction without reflection, and the opposite in which I question the meaning of things. Because of this I have often asked myself why I perform in shows rather than ride in competition, or even do something quite different not involving horses.

I used to worry about whether the things I did were useful and made sense for me, for others, and for the horses. It has taken me some time to understand that a show, apart from being a momentary distraction or an example of technical excellence, could also give meaning to life, both for the person performing and the person watching it. Nowadays, it gives me great satisfaction to feel I have two fundamental aims: to do things well and to do good to others.

I love applause. I used to worry that this was a form of vanity but I now see it as recognition of the work we do; I see it as a way in which the audience shows its enthusiasm for a shared pleasure, and expresses itself in a way that is full of energy and emotion.

These are the moments that make it all worthwhile and give me the sense of doing something useful. The paradox is that if I concentrate on achieving this communication, the magic is suddenly lost. It has taught me that when an artist is painting a picture, he has to concentrate wholly on what he is doing and not be thinking about whether the result will please the public. An act in a show achieves its full impact when I am absorbed in the moment of carrying it out, in the pleasure that it gives to me and to the horse. It is not the moment to be considering whether it is pleasing the public or whether they will learn anything from what they see.

Frédéric Pignon

Keyword:
TALENT

With the public, as with the horses, my object is to be totally committed. I have to clear my mind of worries, thoughts of daily life, of my ego, and of all outside pressures so that my whole being is devoted to the moment.

There is no exchange of magic when I hold back in any way, if I do not give 100 percent of my energy and attention. When I succeed, I get back a response from the public that is made up of sheer joy, laughter, and tears. They open their hearts to me and, for a moment, let me touch their innermost souls. I hope they are connecting with their roots again, with simple pleasures like walking barefoot and enjoying horsey odors. If this is so, I myself am overcome with happiness.

Magali Delgado

Every one of these magnificent stallions was born into the Delgado family stud and trained in a loving atmosphere. There can be few family studs that provide such a fine selection of horses with such charisma and talent, let alone a group of people who think and breathe like horses. They are in the true sense of the word "horse people."

From left to right:
Estelle Delgado, Magali's younger sister, who also takes part in the shows, riding Unico. Their parents, Joelle and Pierrot Delgado, who in their day were trick riders and stunt experts, are riding Jao and Lyrico. Magali is on Galito, and Frédéric on Makao.

Letter to
Our Loved Ones!

Who in the world has had our good fortune to be born into a family whose love for their fellow humans and for animals has played such a key role?

You, our parents, have always given us the courage to follow our dreams and not to fear setbacks. From earliest childhood, you showed your faith in us, whether Magali was entering competitions or I trying to pursue the life of an artist. You only wanted us to be happy. Without the incredible energy and dedication of Magali's parents and the understanding and trust of Frédéric's our lives might have turned out very differently.

We are so thankful to you, Pierrot and Joelle Delgado, that you and the family farm gave us the chance to work with horses, and that you encouraged us to enter competitions and shows. By working with the stud's horses every day, we learned to love and treat them respectfully, and from you, Joelle, we learned about all the herbs and natural medicines that can be used for healing. From you, Pierrot, we found all the support we needed to rise to the top level of the dressage world. When we stumbled, your energy was there to support us. Your belief in us never wavered. Also, you have never wavered for one moment in your own self-belief. You have not allowed others to deflect you from what you believe to be right and by this you have been a constant shining example for us to follow.

At the same time, we thank you, Bernadette and Andre Pignon, for guiding my brother and me toward a new way of treating horses. At a time when people were only interested in the techniques of getting the best results from horses, you showed us that every single horse was different and must be treated with respect for his uniqueness and his place within the herd. You instilled in us the belief that horses are wonderful creatures to be treated with the same respect as people, and so you set us on the path toward discovering a new way of communicating, working, and living with them. In that we have so far succeeded. We owe much to you.

Magali and Frédéric

Three dun colored stallions all with the same sire from the Delgado Stud.

All in harmony with their riders who, in turn, are closely connected to each other.

Frédéric on Nacarado, Magali on her beloved Mandarin, and Estelle on Malicio.

Three horses in one picture demonstrating the three phases of the gallop.

The stallion Nacarado can also be seen in chapter 5 with the stallion Gracil working with Frédéric at liberty.

LINDA TELLINGTON-JONES

As a child I was already searching for this special relationship between human and horse. What intrigued me was the method by which I could come to an understanding between the two species at a deep level. I call this PIC: Profound Interspecies Connections It seemed to me, even then, that the accepted methods of achieving domination by endless repetition had the effect of desensitizing the horse. Sadly, it is still the most common approach to horse training. My vision was to establish a loving relationship that would bring as much joy to the horse as to the rider. It was truly a gift from God that I met two people, Frédéric Pignon and Magali Delgado, who share the same vision. They have not only become close friends but they are brilliant examples of PIC. I first caught sight of Frédéric at the world famous horse expo, Equitana in Essen, Germany, where he was giving a display of freedom dressage. I knew immediately that I had to get to know him.

I had never seen anything like Frédéric's demonstration: a man playing with a stallion that was exploding with energy and all at total liberty. They danced together, leaped into the air, played games with each other, and then at the end, the stallion came over to Frédéric and laid his head on the man's shoulder. Never had I seen a stallion that was completely free and happy and wanted to work with a man. At the very least, stallions are always muzzled so that they do not go off and bite other stallions. But with Frédéric it was different. The stallion was enjoying every second of the performance, and what radiated from Frédéric captivated every person in the audience as much as it did the horse. His connection with the horse was so tangible that the two seemed to be one.

Magali Delgado, Frédéric's wife, is another example of someone with this special connection to a horse. On the same day, after winning the top prize at the Grand Prix dressage, she demonstrated all the same movements but without saddle or bridle, just a rope lying loosely around the horse's neck. She appeared as light as a feather, the horse was completely unstressed, and showed no sign of tiredness, and the joy that radiated from both was so remarkable I could not drag my eyes away from them. My heart too leaped with joy.

When I went to seek them out, I had no idea if Frédéric and Magali would be interested in my Tellington TTouch Method. However, I knew that it could help them if a horse was suffering from stress—almost inevitable when traveling and living in unfamiliar stalls. To my delight they were interested and I soon had the chance to demonstrate the TTouch's effectiveness. While they were in the middle of the *Cavalia* shows on the U.S. circuit, Frédéric asked me to have a look at Fasto who appeared to be suffering from stress. We made our way to his stall. We still laugh when we recall Frédéric's first reaction to the encounter. I asked him to put a halter on the horse so that I could work on his ears. Fred knew that Fasto hated his ears being touched by anyone, let alone by a little woman he had never met before. But this is what happened and it is always the same whenever I work with a horse. With-

in a minute or two, the stallion was standing quite still; he lowered his head and allowed me to put one hand on his nose and the other on his ears, which I began to stroke from the roots to the tips. This is the very best way to calm a horse in the shortest possible time: so that he eats his food, becomes animated again or, as was in this case, prepared for a show.

This was a first step toward a deep friendship between us and Frédéric and Magali's horses. Still today, that friendship plays an important part in my life.

Whenever Roland, my husband, and I need to relax, or find new energy and inspiration, we go to visit Frédéric and Magali in the south of France. Occasionally, we also meet at expos and delight in their company.

Frédéric calls me his "fairy godmother" because, whenever he really needs me, I seem

to appear. Thus it was that I turned up in San Francisco when he was about to put on a spectacular show with *Cavalia*. It gave me the opportunity to give the riders and the horses' minders a demonstration of the TTouch that put all the horses in the right frame of mind for their performance.

In the following year we met in Dallas, Texas, where Frédéric began to use the Mouth TTouch whenever he needed to calm a stallion. Phoebus, the younger of the two Friesian stallions, was feeling cowed by the more dominant Paulus. On one occasion, Phoebus tried to bite Paulus at a show, so Frédéric kept Phoebus in the arena under the spotlight in order to give him a very short, but effective treatment, of this TTouch.

I've been teaching this Method for years but I have never come across anyone who picked it up so effectively as Frédéric. The technique consists of using the TTouch to massage the mouth, which connects directly with the emotional center in the brain, the lymphatic system. The desire to bite is brought on by stress and anxiety but when you induce a state of relaxed attention by gently massaging the nostrils and lower lip, it is possible to reduce the level of stress very quickly. I had shown Frédéric how to use his fingers to circulate round the jaw muscles, and Frédéric understood immediately that even he could achieve a marked change and stop the biting by using the technique for a few seconds. Since that in-

cident, the Mouth TTouch has become a key element in his training program and so effectively does he use it that since then I have called it the "Fred-TTouch"!

In an interview at *Equitana* in March 2013, Magali told the story of how she had used TTouches to calm the stallions before the curtain went up and the show began. She had not yet used the technique so the stallions were in a state of high excitement, knowing that at any moment they would erupt into the arena and be at a full gallop under the spotlights. In this way, she discovered how easy it was to keep the stallions calm, so much so that she had to use it with discretion because they could be so calm that they missed their entrance!

On my first visit to Frédéric and Magali's training centre in Avignon, my husband, Roland, and I were traveling with our friend,

115

Gabriele Boiselle. It was then that I had the pleasure of working with Gracil for the first time: While we were walking through the barn, being presented to the horses, my interest was aroused by a young stallion that had only recently arrived and was still feeling like a stranger. This was Gracil. I told Frédéric I would like to spend some time with him; at that moment I didn't know that Frédéric had as yet done very little with him, and not yet decided whether to add him to the show horses because the horse still lacked trust in humans. I stood absolutely still in the stall until Gracil turned his head toward me. Without even putting a halter on him I began to give him gentle TTouches, first on his shoulder and then on his back, moving finally to his rear legs. He stood perfectly still. Finally, I could lay my arm behind his ears, a position of total trust. On another visit, we all celebrated the publication of the first book about Frédéric and Magali, *Gallop to Freedom*, just published in English. In our little group, together with Roland and Gabriele, the dogs, and a stallion that was freely grazing nearby, the champagne corks popped, and we all brimmed with happiness. Not far away, the stallions were grazing in their paddock that was only separated from us by a single electric wire fence.

We had only just sat down at the large table in the garden to toast the success of the book when we heard the shrill and agitated neighing of a stallion, openly challenging his neighbor that happened to be Magali's Mandarin. Both stallions were galloping along the length of the wire and it would only have been a matter of seconds before one of them had knocked it down. We had the time to look up at what was happening but Frédéric had already sprung to his feet and placed himself between the two stallions. What passed between them is not easy to describe. It was as if Frédéric had been able to harness the electricity in the wire: Assuming the stooped posture of a predator, he fixed the young stallion with his look. He mirrored the stallion's body language, seemed to absorb or block the aggression, and succeeded in establishing a connection without upsetting him.

Mandarin was totally concentrated on Frédéric, even though he was still trembling with the commotion and rush of testosterone; Frédéric was able to approach him and put a rope around his neck. Without raising his voice, he praised the horse that by now was walking beside him, totally under his emotional control. It was the most impressive demonstration of non-verbal communication and of a deep bond that I have ever witnessed.

On several occasions I had spoken to Frédéric and Magali about the possibility of holding a joint seminar where we would demonstrate my methods combined with their magic. In 2012 we managed it: 100 horse enthusiasts from five different countries came together. Twice a day, Frédéric taught eight riders how to work with his stallions and, among other things, they worked on Spanish Step. Magali gave riding lessons in the outdoor arena and I worked on four horses demonstrating the TTouch. At the end of the two days everyone went home with something to try out on their own horses.

What really struck me during this weekend was how Frédéric worked for hours in a completely peaceful and clear manner. It seems to me he has a clear picture in his mind of what he wants the horse to do and how he will look given his potential, and when he understands what is wanted and is performing it. When he looks at a horse with his inner eye, he sees only perfection. His work is entirely based on love and re-

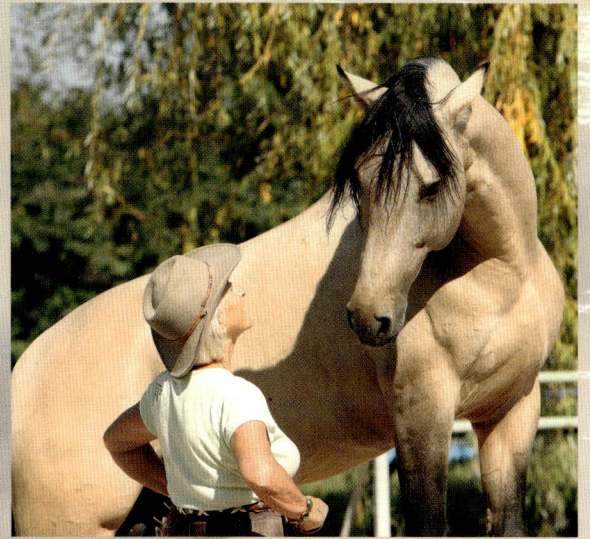

spect and the horses feel this and place their trust in him.

I try to avoid using the word "love" because it is all too often misused, but when I see Frédéric at the close of the seminar telling people that a successful relationship with a horse has to be based on love, I can find no other word that will suffice. If you have trouble with "love" you can try replacing it with "high regard" but it is not really satisfactory. You should see Magali working with students, or being with her son Noah, or with her friends, or with Frédéric, or indeed with the horses. Love is the only word that really suffices. They are marvelous with their horses but what they demonstrate in addition is their thankfulness for all the blessings of their life. They have both stared death in the face and are all the more determined to share their love with those around them as well as with the horses. This is a huge gift to all who come into contact with them.

117

DAVID WALSER

Afterword

I had the great pleasure of writing *Gallop to Freedom* with Magali and Frédéric in 2009 so when Trafalgar Square Books asked me to translate this new book I feared I might not find it as interesting as working directly with them and actually writing *Gallop to Freedom*. However, when I saw Gabriele's photographs and read Magali and Frédéric's explanations of how they go about their work, I felt inspired and moved all over again.

I see now that when I first met them in 2008, they were approaching the end of their connection with *Cavalia* and, as we learn in this book, Frédéric was going through a period of self-examination. All those performances I witnessed in the capitals of Europe a few years ago seemed utterly magical but I see that as a result of a period of re-evaluation the shows must now have reached a new plane of achievement in that he allows so much freedom to his horses in every performance.

When I first knew them, Frédéric told me that every now and then a horse would tell him what he wanted to perform as they were going on stage—this had been the case with Templado fairly frequently. It sounded almost incredible to me but as Frédéric explains in this book, he has now made it the norm to encourage every horse he works with "at freedom" to be creative and make suggestions; it's truly an extraordinary achievement. Frédéric and Magali have both in their own way achieved a symbiotic relationship with horses that is so close, loving, and fruitful that I wonder if we shall ever see the like.

In a way, this book could almost have been published without text: the photographs are so revealing that they tell the story without the need of words. The photographs are like poetry and transmit the love and respect that flows in both directions between man and horse. But perhaps we are not sufficiently educated in the art of observation, so words are still necessary to help us along.

It is also very moving to hear Frédéric and Magali telling of their experiences and their philosophy. They both have a highly developed ability to read the body language of a horse and, perhaps, of people. This book gives us an opportunity to really look at each photograph and try to understand what is being transmitted. Of course, a photograph tells us less than real life but it is a start, and perhaps when we next look at a horse—or a person, too—it will be with new eyes.